Paws in the Cots~~~~~~

While the pubs featured in this book were dog-friendly at the time of visiting, changes of ownership or other circumstances may mean that dogs are no longer welcome.

To ensure your dog is welcome and that the pub is open on the day you plan to visit, you are advised to phone and check before setting out. There is contact information at the end of the book.

The author and the publisher have done their best to ensure that the information in this book is accurate at the time of printing, but cannot be held responsible for errors or inaccuracies.

Readers should keep to public rights of way at all times, and the description of land, a building, a path or another feature in this book is not evidence of a right of way or other public access.

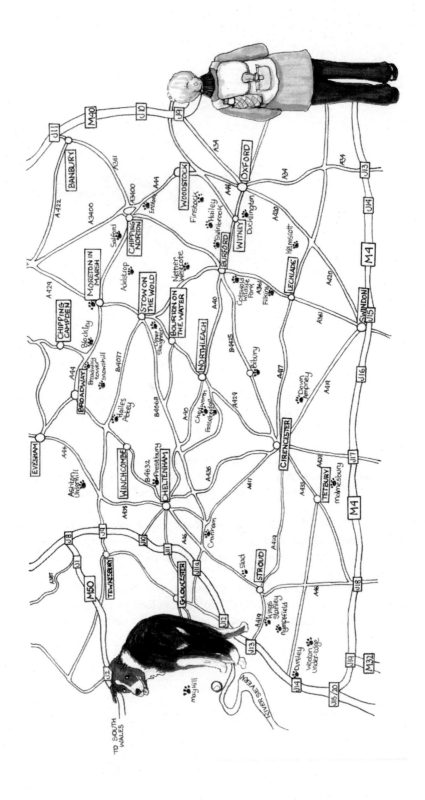

Paws in the Cotswolds

Helen Peacocke

Illustrated by Sue Mynall

Photographs by the author

THE WYCHWOOD PRESS

Dedication

Pythius would like to raise his paws in praise of Roy and Kate Cooper who have patiently edited all his scripts which, as he admits, are often in need of correction. His mistress Helen says it is because his paws don't always hit the right keys when he's typing, but Pythius knows it's because he is a Border collie and Border collies can't always spell correctly, especially when they're anxiously waiting for their next walk.

Walk the Cotswold countryside with a dog faithfully plodding beside you as you explore the Gloucestershire hills and valleys and you will experience a companionship second to none.

Anon

Our books may be ordered from bookshops or (post free) from
The Wychwood Press, Alder House, Market Street, Charlbury, OX7 3PH
01608 819117

e-mail: jon@evenlodebooks.co.uk

First published in 2012 by
The Wychwood Press
an imprint of Jon Carpenter Publishing
Alder House, Market Street, Charlbury, Oxfordshire OX7 3PH

The right of Helen Peacocke to be identified as author of this work has been asserted in accordance with the Copyright, Designs and Patents Act 1988

The right of Sue Mynall to be identified as creator of the drawings and the map in this work has been asserted in accordance with the Copyright, Designs and Patents Act 1988

ISBN 978 1 902279 46 6

Printed in England by CPI Antony Rowe Ltd., Chippenham SN14 6LH

Contents

The Cotswolds: an introduction 7

Adlestrop : The Fox, Lower Oddington

    Edward Thomas and Jane Austen 9

Batsford Arboretum : The Crown Inn, Blockley

    Mitford sisters' territory 12

Bibury : The Catherine Wheel

    A gentle amble round the grounds of Bibury Trout Farm 15

Bredon Hil l: The Star Inn, Ashton under Hill

    A walk on Bredon Hill inspired by the poet A. E. Housman 18

Broadway Tower : Morris & Brown at the Tower

    To the top of Broadway Tower and back 22

Burford : Cotswold Wildlife Park

    The Royal Oak 26

Chedworth Roman Villa : The Seven Tuns

    Three mile circular walk 29

Cranham : The Black Horse

    Walking with Gustav Holst 32

Down Ampney : The Old Spotted Cow, Marston Meysey

    Walking in the footsteps of Ralph Vaughan Williams 35

Ducklington : The Bell

    A two-mile river walk in the childhood home of Mollie Harris 38

Dursley, Stinchcombe Hill : The Inn

    A walk along the Cotswold Way and Korea Friendship Trail 41

Enstone : The Crown, Church Enstone

    In the footsteps of farm worker Mont Abbott 44

Farmcote : Hailes Abbey, Farmcote Herbs and Chilli Pepper Farm

    Two-mile walk 48

Filkins : The Five Alls

    A walk from the Cotswold Woollen Weavers Heritage Centre 51

Finstock : The Plough Inn

    A walk taking in the church in which T. S. Eliot was baptised 54

Fossebridge : The Inn at Fossebridge

    The Fosse Way: a Roman road. An idyllic walk 58

May Hill : The Yew Tree, Cliffords Mesne

    Celebrating Ivor Gurney, Cotswold composer and poet 61

Kelmscott : The Plough

    Walking in the footsteps of William Morris   65

King's Stanley: The King's Head

    The artist Sir Stanley Spencer and the village of Leonard Stanley   68

Malmesbury : The Smoking Dog

    Looking out for Eilmer the flying monk   72

Minster Lovell : The Old Swan

    Walk to the ruins of Mister Lovell Hall   75

Moreton-in-Marsh : The Bell Inn

    A drink in the original for Tolkien's 'Prancing Pony'   75

Nether Westcote : The Feathered Nest Inn

    Circular walk taking in two ancient ridge and furrow fields   83

Nympsfield : The Rose and Crown Inn

    A little bit of Archers' fantasy   87

Ozleworth : The Royal Oak, Wotton under Edge

    Healthy wild garlic in a valley J. B. Priestley loved   91

Prestbury : The Plough Inn

    Circular walk round the most haunted village in Gloucestershire   94

Salford : The Black Horse

    Four miles to the Rollright Stones and back   98

Slad : The Woolpack

    A circular walk through Laurie Lee country   102

Snowshill Lavender Fields : three dog-friendly pubs   107

Swinbrook : The Swan Inn

    A two-mile river walk in the footsteps of the Mitford sisters   110

Upper Slaughter : The Lords of the Manor

    Along the Warden's way to Lower Slaughter and back   113

Pythius' Epilogue   117

Contact information   118

The Cotswolds
An Introduction

The rolling green hills, valleys, babbling streams and rose-covered stone cottages of the Cotswolds have influenced the lives of many great men and women over the centuries, and in turn artists such as William Morris have left their mark on this quintessentially English area that is justifiably designated an Area of Outstanding Beauty.

The Cotswold landscape has also been moulded by successive generations of farmers and their stock, stone wallers, who built the many dry stone walls that criss-cross the countryside, and stone masons, who built the great wool churches, artisans' grand homes and humble cottages from local stone that cluster together, forming picturesque little villages and market towns.

If these remarks have not yet convinced you that, as J. B. Priestley once wrote, 'The Cotswolds are the most English and the least spoiled of all our countrysides,' then read on. The aim of this little book is to inspire you to get out into this glorious region that stretches from Chipping Campden in the north to Bath in the south, visit the remote valleys and hills that have inspired poets, composers and artists, and embrace the exceptional beauty of this area for yourselves.

I have walked the Cotswolds in the company of my beloved Border collie Pythius and friends, and rejoice in the unspoiled nature of this area. Earlier Paws books spanned Oxfordshire and the Cotswolds, but gradually as we all grew to know the Cotswolds better, the idea for this book developed from a whim to reality. Oxfordshire is still included but only where the destination falls under the Cotswold classification.

Helen Peacocke

Pythius has his say

Every week now (come rain or shine) my mistress Helen and her friend Auntie Liz bundle me into her ancient Mini and head for the Cotswolds. This trip is the highlight of my week. First we visit a dog-friendly pub for lunch, then spend the rest of the day exploring, sometimes walking in the footsteps of famous men and women who trod that way before.

Because the landscape of the Cotswolds is so varied, I never know quite what to expect. Sometimes we just wander among gently rolling hills and along winding green lanes, or follow the dramatic landscape of the scarp on the Cotswoldsí western edge.

I must admit that as the 'girls' are getting on a bit, they do struggle with some of the steep climbs, but on reaching the edge of the scarp the view stretched out before them always takes their breath away. Mine too. The views can be mesmerising; such that all we can do is stand and stare. It's as if the entire world is stretched out before us, lush, green and beautiful, with rivers of crisp clear water rippling gently through the folds of the hills.

As the Cotswolds are a doggie paradise, I reckon I am the luckiest Border collie in the whole wide world.

The rules I have to follow:

Once the walk has begun I have to stay under close control at all times, most particularly when walking a bridle way or byway in case we meet a horse. Helen says she's responsible and I might frighten the horses and cause an accident.

I must be on a lead or under close control when we approach farm animals too. Apparently the farmer has a right to destroy any dog that injures or worries the animals.

I must not jump over walls, or rush through holes in hedges and must wait patiently while Helen closes farm gates securely once we have passed through them.

I am not allowed to wander into areas where ground-nesting birds are nesting, particularly between March 1 and July 31, as vulnerable species such as skylarks can be easily disturbed if I don't stick to the footpath.

I must always wait for her to put me on the lead when we approach a road and must never dart out into the road without her.

Rules that Helen has to follow when I am accompanying her:

She must always keep a bottle of cold water in the car and provide me with a drink of water whenever I need one.

She must never, EVER, shut me in the car on a warm day and leave me there while she goes shopping

She must strap me into my doggie-safety harness whenever we go for a drive.

Adlestrop
The Fox, Lower Oddington

Edward Thomas and Jane Austen

A two-mile walk through Adlestrop

Upper and Lower Oddington are two picturesque little Cotswold villages that are reached by turning off the A436 road that runs from Burford to Stow-on the-Wold. They lie just three miles east of Stow-on-the-Wold amid the most beautiful undulating countryside and close to Adlestrop, which was made famous by the war poet Edward Thomas who was moved to write of his experience when the express train he was travelling on stopped momentarily at Adlestrop station.

> *Yes, I remember Adlestrop –*
> *The name, because one afternoon*
> *Of heat the express-train drew up there*
> *Unwontedly. It was late June.*
>
> *The steam hissed. Someone cleared his throat.*
> *No one left and no one came*
> *On the bare platform. What I saw*
> *Was Adlestrop – only the name ...*

As a result of railway closures in the 1960s, the station he speaks of no longer exists, though the track is still in use. A railway bench on the edge of the village and the original Adlestrop sign commemorate this poem which is engraved on a small brass plaque for all to enjoy.

Jane Austen is also linked with Adlestrop as she was related to Reverend Thomas Leigh who lived there. She is said to have visited him at least three times and worshipped in his church, St Mary Magdalene, staying in the rectory directly opposite the church.

The Fox Inn, Lower Oddington

During the autumn this 16th-century pub, with its traditional cottage garden, is easy to spot as it lies in the centre of the village and is clad with Virginia creepers that transform the building into a furnace that

glows red during the autumn months. Inside you walk over polished flagstone floors and under thick oak beams, past antique furniture and a series of small cosy rooms which are stylishly laid ready for diners. Starched white linen napkins give an indication of the kind of pub this is, yet despite its stylish appearance and comforting atmosphere, dogs are very welcome. The selection of beer is impressive and includes local brews from the nearby Hook Norton Brewery.

Pythius loves this pub; the staff treat him with respect and they don't seem to mind at all if he trots off to find a suitable table to place his paws under. The food is not cheap, but this inn is known for its imaginative menu and you can have a very reasonable and very tasty meal if you choose carefully as vegetables and bread are included in the main meal price. A glistening metal jug of iced water is placed on the table the moment you sit down, which adds a great touch to the meal experience and something visitors appear to remember long after they have left. I have never seen a more striking water jug.

The Walk

You can walk from Lower Oddington to Adlestrop by turning left on leaving the pub and left again when you reach the junction that links the main street with the A436.

But first take a few moments to explore the nearby 11th-century St Nicholas parish church just a quarter-of-a-mile walk from the pub. Look for the signpost to the right of the pub and take Church Lane, which will lead you down a glorious wooded path to the church. Here is one of the largest medieval 'doom' wall paintings in the country which takes up most of the north wall. Return to the pub and either

> **Pythius says**
>
> Exploring two churches and just gently trotting through two pretty little villages is not a dog's idea of a real walk, but that said, it seemed to please Auntie Liz and Helen, and if they are happy, I am happy. Besides – I love visiting the Fox – a really stylish old inn that knows how to keep a dog happy.

walk onto Adlestrop which is just a mile away, or drive to the Adlestrop church hall car park which is close to the railway bench commemorating Thomas's poem, one of the great poems of the 20th century.

Now amble gently along the main street of this glorious little village and soak up the atmosphere generated by honey-coloured stone cottages and its thatched post office – and imagine that you are walking in Jane Austen's footsteps as you make your way to the church of St Mary Magdalene. You will find the church down a little lane on the right-hand side of the main street at the far end of the village. Having passed through its cast iron entry gate, take a moment to enjoy its rural setting, which is as tranquil as the countryside which surrounds this parish church. The oldest part is the 13th-century chancel arch, though we were overcome by the fact that Jane Austen would have sat in one of the pews – but which one? We had fun guessing.

Walk on down the green lane to a gate which leads to Adlestrop Park. It is rumoured that both the grounds and house of Adlestrop Park were the setting for the novel *Mansfield Park*.

As sheep are often grazing in the park, keep your dog under close control or on its lead as you walk round the grounds, turning back along the lane when you are ready to return to the car park. This walk is not long, but it's relaxing, and remember you are walking in Jane Austen's footsteps.

Batsford Arboretum

The Crown Inn, Blockley

Mitford sisters' territory

This walk can be as short or as long as you want

Tucked away off the A44 just a couple of miles from Moreton-in-Marsh, Gloucestershire, Batsford Arboretum is called the Cotswolds' Secret Garden. Here you are free to amble round the grounds and view the 1,300 different species of trees and shrubs and enjoy some breathtaking views of the Cotswold countryside. Whilst the emphasis at this arboretum is greatly influenced by the Far East, there is a great variety of native species too.

It was during the 1860s that Algernon Bertram Freeman-Mitford, 1st Baron Redesdale, inherited the estate from John Thomas Freeman-Mitford, his first cousin twice removed. Algernon, known as 'Barty', had travelled throughout oriental Asia as an attaché to the foreign legation, and was heavily influenced by the plants he had seen there,

particularly the bamboos. He demolished the Georgian House in the grounds and rebuilt a new mansion during the late 1880s and set about creating a 'wild' garden of near natural plantings inspired by his observations of plant groupings in the Japanese landscape.

When he died he was succeeded by his second son David, father of the infamous Mitford sisters, who lived there during the first world war. Nancy, the eldest daughter, based the early part of her popular novel *Love in a Cold Climate* on their time in Batsford.

Unfortunately dogs have to remain on their leads throughout their visit here, but if your dog can cope with that, a visit to this beautiful place will be really rewarding, especially during autumn.

We try to visit during mid-October when the maples provide a rich mix of red and golden leaves that weave a magic flame-like hue between the Sorbus collection of brightly coloured autumn foliage and berries and the blaze of orange, purple, bronze and red leaves of the flowering cherries.

This is a peaceful place. Even Pythius senses it as we walk along the twisting walkways, past the giant redwoods that attempt to reach the sky and the various sculptures scattered throughout the grounds. As a generous supply of seats and benches are strategically placed to enable visitors to relax during their visit and enjoy the views, elderly visitors are amply catered for. So are wheelchair users who are allowed in free. Wheelchairs can be reserved if ordered in advance, to save having to pack them into your car.

There is a falconry attached to the arboretum, but Pythius was not allowed in there. He didn't mind that. He's not really into birds and indeed might have been scared if they swooped too close to his head.

A new restaurant has been constructed recently, complete with gift shop. This gets very busy as the food is good, but there is plenty of room outside where visitors can sit in a marquee to enjoy their lunch. It is not licensed, so Pythius was unable to enjoy the aroma of malt from our beer as we drank soft drinks, while he sipped water from a bowl supplied for canine visitors. That was fine, he coped with that too. In fact, given he was on a lead all the time during our visit to Batsford, he managed this trip very well.

Pythius says:

Well – I was given a choice. Either stay at home while Auntie Caroline and Helen went to the arboretum, or comply with the rules that demand dogs are kept on their leads. I have to laugh at this directive, for although it says I must be on a lead, it never says that a human should be holding the lead. Sometimes, when she thinks she can get away with it, Helen lets go of the lead and allows me to wander free for a moment or two, because she also recognises she is still obeying the rules if she does so. But she never does this when visiting places like the arboretum.

We ate lunch outside in the sun this time, on a table close to a marquee. The girls seemed to enjoy that. I was tied to the table and spent most of the time talking to other dogs who were also coping with restrictions imposed on us. All in all it was a very pleasant day. I certainly enjoyed the crunchy fallen leaves underfoot and spent some time talking to the two cats and a hedgehog I encountered during our walk, who all roamed free without the constraints of a lead.

Had we wanted a more substantial lunch and an alcoholic drink, we could have left the arboretum and travelled just a couple of miles to Blockley, an exceptionally beautiful Cotswold village built mainly on a series of terraces. Here you will discover the 17th-century Crown Inn hotel which stands in the centre of the village. If you feel particularly energetic, you can walk to Blockley along the Monarch's Way, but as this path leads you through several fields of grazing sheep, your dog will have to remain on the lead.

The Crown Inn is stylishly decorated in a manner that has allowed it to retain its rustic charm, and dogs are welcomed with open arms. Pythius enjoys visiting this inn. He is not allowed in the restaurant, but there is plenty of room in the front bar for him to place his paws under the table, while we enjoy selecting home-cooked food at affordable prices created from local produce. A good selection of local ales is also on tap. In other words, it is a very welcoming hostelry in which to lunch after spending the morning at the arboretum.

Bibury
The Catherine Wheel

A gentle amble round the grounds of Bibury Trout Farm

William Morris described Bibury as the most beautiful village in England. Having visited this charming little Cotswold town in all its guises, I'm inclined to agree, though I think I like it best during the winter months when it is not clogged up with tourists. I wonder what he would say if he were able to see it now during the height of the tourist season?

Most tourists come armed with cameras to photograph the famous Arlington Row, said to be the most photographed scene in the country. These picturesque cottages were originally built as a monastic wool store in 1380 and converted into homes for weavers during the 17th century. They are now in the safe hands of the National Trust.

Tourists are also attracted to Bibury's Trout Farm, which can be found in the centre of town close to the Swan Inn and beside the little bridge that spans the River Coln.

Founded in 1902 by naturalist Arthur Seven to stock local rivers and

streams with native brown trout, its 15 acres of grounds are now open to visitors. Apart from walking the grounds, visitors can view and feed the fish, even catch their own if they wish, or buy fresh and smoked trout from the fish shop which is also stocked with an excellent selection of wine, artisan bread and other tasty goodies. It is a great place to visit particularly as dogs are permitted entry providing they remain on a lead. The tea shop has outside seating, enabling customers to soak up the atmosphere of this splendid Cotswold amenity on a sunny day.

The Catherine Wheel Inn

This charming pub with its low beams and stone walls dates back to the 15th century and was once the home of a wheelwright, also a cooper, who not only made beer barrels but sold beer too. Nailsworth Brewery took it over in 1899. Like so many Cotswold inns it has been tastefully brought into the 21st century in a manner which has not destroyed its 15th century charm.

One of the advantages of visiting this inn is its spacious car park. Trying to find somewhere to park your car when visiting Bibury for lunch during the summer months is never easy, so this is a real bonus. The Catherine Wheel boasts a spacious wooded garden too.

During the winter months the Catherine Wheel usually offers a two course lunch at a very competitive price, which given that everything is cooked from scratch by a very professional chef, proves a real bargain. On our last visit the lunch, which included fishcakes created from Bibury trout, proved so delicious we decided to finish it off with a portion of home-made ice cream decorated with crunchy brandy snaps for good measure. If you have never tasted home-made chocolate ice cream, may I encourage you to give it a try. You won't regret ordering it.

There's a good assortment of local real ales too, and Pythius's water arrived in a lovely terracotta bowl.

The staff are simply charming, so willing to do whatever is needed to ensure your stay is agreeable. In the summer when they have to deal with people eating in the garden as well as its restaurant and two charming little bar areas, they are amazing. Even when this pub is really crowded I have never had to wait long for my meal.

Obviously Pythius is not allowed in the restaurant area, but he is able to make himself comfortable and stretch out in front of the fire in the bar areas when we have our lunch. He loves visiting this pub.

Pythius Says

When that red leather lead comes out of Helen's pocket and she commands me to sit, I know the walk isn't going to be everything I wish for. And a walk through a fish farm – what self-respecting dog wants anything to do with fish? Fish is for cats, not Border collies!

The pub is charming. When we visit during the winter I get to warm myself besides the fire, and in the summer I can sit in the shade of the trees.

The walk through the trout farm

There is a small charge to visit the grounds of the trout farm, but if you have children with you who would enjoy throwing fish food into the water, then watch as the trout leap up to catch it, it's a small price to pay. There is a small area specially designed for children with climbing frame and other play things.

Pythius gave a silent groan when he realised that he was not going to be let off his lead as we walked round the fish ponds and admired the ducks. He got used to it however, as he always does. In fact he was fascinated when he saw the trout leap up for the food I threw into the water.

Yes, there was a tricky moment when Pythius wondered if he should jump in too and catch some of the little pellets before they fell into the water. Fortunately Auntie Liz had him firmly in control, so nothing untoward happened and the fish caught the pellets long before Pythius could get anywhere near them.

The farm consists of 41 acres of grounds. At any one time there will be more than twenty thousand trout in various stages of their development, swimming the waters of the farm. Many will be transported live to restock rivers and lakes throughout the UK, while the rest find themselves in the kitchens of nearby hostelries, where fresh Bibury trout is much prized, or in the little shop attached to the farm which enables visitors to purchase glistening fresh trout at its very best.

Bredon Hill
The Star Inn, Ashton under Hill

A two-mile walk on Bredon Hill inspired by the poet A. E. Housman

> *In summertime on Bredon*
> *The bells they sound so clear;*
> *Round both round the shires they ring them*
> *In steeples far and near,*
> *A happy noise to hear.*
>
> *Here on a Sunday morning*
> *My love and I would lie,*
> *And see the coloured counties*
> *And hear the larks so high*
> *About us in the sky ...*
>
> Extract from A. E. Housman's 1896 anthology A Shropshire Lad

We climbed Bredon Hill during January, so sadly there were no skylarks flying overhead and bare branches added very little colour to the counties scattered below: it was nevertheless an exhilarating experience, particularly as the hill is one of the most important wildlife sites in England.

Bredon Hill is 14 miles south-west of Evesham and although it is geologically part of the Cotswolds and lies within the Cotswolds Area of Outstanding Natural Beauty, as a result of erosion over millions of years it now stands isolated in the Vale of Evesham.

Parson's Folly, an 18th-century tower built at its summit, adds the necessary 19 feet to bring its height to a full 1,000 feet. This walk/climb therefore, is not for the faint-hearted, unless of course you do as we did and take the gentle dip slope from Ashton under Hill and climb to the top of the Great Hill which is one of several hills on Bredon.

It wasn't just Housman who immortalised this hill. Bredon Hill has long exerted a strange magnetism on those that climb its slopes and the inhabitants of the villages that encircle it. It is a mysterious place that tugs you like an impatient companion as you aim to reach its summit to enjoy the panoramic views it promises.

Over the centuries it has attracted a multitude of composers, poets, writers and artists, including Ralph Vaughan Williams, Ivor Gurney, Cecil Day-Lewis and William Cobbett. We were, therefore, walking in the footsteps of many creative men, as well as our ancient pagan ancestors who had inhabited and shaped the hill since the Bronze Age.

I have always wondered why Housman wove this into *A Shropshire Lad*. Apparently he wrote the poems in this anthology while living in London and before ever visiting Shropshire. As he was born in Fockbury near Bromsgrove, Worcestershire, less than 30 miles away, no doubt he walked Bredon when young and called on youthful memories for his poem? Well that's what I would like to think.

The Star Inn, Ashton under Hill

The Star Inn nestles under Bredon Hill, standing a little way back from Elmley Road that runs through Ashton under Hill. Because many of the customers are walkers, you will probably find several pairs of muddy boots stacked carefully inside the main entrance.

Dogs are allowed in the main bar area but not the restaurant. On the day we visited this inn there were almost a dozen dogs with their paws under the tables. It was so crowded with exhausted canines who, like us, had just climbed the hill, we had to search for a table in the small adjoining room on the left.

As this atmospheric little pub closes at 3 pm and doesn't serve food on Monday and Sunday evenings, it is worth timing your walk so you arrive before it shuts its doors. Several real ales are on offer – we went for Black Sheep which proved particularly satisfying. Water was brought for Pythius the moment we requested it. As there were no rivers on the hill, and he didn't find the muddy puddles we passed very tasty, he drank it enthusiastically, then put his head down and went to sleep while we munched our way through a couple of baguettes filled with steak slices. As all the meat cooked at the Star Inn is locally sourced, we ate with confidence.

We certainly enjoyed our time there as other like-minded walkers sitting close to us were eager to talk about their walk and discuss the many trips they had taken up Bredon Hill. It was all very companionable.

The walk

We began by walking through the lychgate and churchyard of St Barbara's church just a few yards from the pub and made our way through a couple of kissing gates into a meadow. We then began to climb to the right hand corner of the field that leads to steps that took us to Bakers Lane. Having crossed the lane and climbed a stile, from thereon we just followed the marker posts for the Wychavon Way that crosses Bredon Hill. We were walking onto the hilltop known as the

Pythius says

My task while walking Bredon Hill was to keep a lookout for the Beast of Bredon, a large black cat who is said to inhabit the hill. What Uncle John and Helen thought I was going to do if I spotted the creature I simply don't know – was I supposed to chase it away, or invite it to approach us? Fortunately the question didn't arise, there was neither sight nor sound of the mysterious creature and I didn't sniff out any witches either, which was another job they had given me. Now what on earth would a Border collie do with a witch?

Great Hill which meant we did not encounter the King and Queen stones – but that's OK, we will return for further walks as Bredon Hill is etched with an abundance of footpaths and bridleways. In fact, you can make a walk up as you go providing you keep to the footpaths, though it is worth taking an Ordnance Survey map with you, if only to ensure you return to the village from which you started.

You will have reached the top of the Great Hill when you get to a substantial wooden gate which leads to a field (of brassicas when we were there) and the chance to walk further by following the signs that guide you round the edge of the field. If you continue to follow the Wychavon Way for a couple of miles it will take you past Castle Hill where the remains of a Norman castle can be seen.

To return from the top of the Great Hill, turn, enjoy the panoramic view laid out before you and aim for the point where the track you took meets another – take the left hand track and go through a metal farm gate into a pasture field, bearing right after just a few yards and then take the steep downhill track to another farm gate and cattle grid, past farm buildings and downhill to Cotton's Lane which leads to Elmley Road. Turn right on reaching this road and it will take you back to your starting point.

You will have walked just two miles, but it may seem more in parts as you are walking uphill on the way out. It's not a difficult climb as such, but it is a climb nevertheless. Be assured the views are worth it, and if you have timed it correctly, a glass of real ale at the Star Inn will restore your energy in seconds.

Broadway Tower

Morris & Brown at the Tower

Three-mile walk to the top of Broadway Tower and back

If you have ever wondered what it would feel like to stand on the top of a high hill on a clear day and look out on a panoramic view that incorporates at least 12 counties – then a walk to the tower on the top of Beacon Hill, Broadway, is definitely for you and your dog.

Broadway, Worcestershire, lies 40 miles west of Oxford. It is close to Stow-on-the-Wold and several other idyllic Cotswold villages, among them Snowshill.

On driving down its ancient High Street, it soon becomes apparent that Broadway really does deserve the title 'Jewel of the Cotswolds' and the 'Show village of England'.

This street, which really is a Broad Way, leads to the foot of the western Cotwolds escarpment and is flanked with the most fascinating assortment of humble cottages, grand Georgian buildings, quaint little shops, old coaching inns dating from the 16th century and red chestnut trees. Classified as the longest High Street in England, it is indeed a Mecca for tourists. Unlike many other Cotswold spots that offer a timeless sense of peace, Broadway is never without visitors.

Its famous hill, about one-and-a-quarter miles south east of the town and known as Beacon Hill, is 1024 feet above sea level, making it the second highest hill on the Cotswold ridge. The magnificent 55-foot high tower that dominates its peak is the perfect example of an 18th-century gothic folly. Famous writers and artists whose names are linked with Broadway and its hill include Henry James, J. M. Barrie, Vaughan Williams, Elgar, John Singer Sargent and William Morris of the Arts and Crafts Movement – many of whom would have undoubtedly walked to the top of Beacon Hill during their association with this area.

The vision for this tower came from Capability Brown, the great landscape designer, but it was George William, 6th Earl of Coventry, and architect James Wyatt who completed it in 1798.

William Morris and members of the Arts and Crafts Movement including Pre-Raphaelite artists Dante Gabriel Rossetti and Edward Burne-Jones used it as a holiday retreat in the 1880s. Actually, it was the town of Broadway and the tower that inspired William Morris to campaign for the preservation of historic monuments, which is why rooms in the tower are now furnished with his popular designs.

The tower has had other uses. Due to its height, it offered a unique vantage point to track enemy planes flying over England during the first and second world wars. During the cold war, a nuclear bunker was incorporated into the tower. Now it is open to visitors throughout the year , except when adverse weather makes this difficult. A small charge is made to ascend its three storeys to enjoy the view, but be assured it is well worth it if you still have the energy after climbing the hill.

The walk

The walk begins by taking a footpath marked THE COTSWOLD WAY AND THE BROADWAY TOWER on a wooden signpost, which you will see on the right-hand side when you walk up the High Street from the centre of town. You will notice other way-signs before you reach this one – ignore them; this is the one you want if you plan a direct route to the top. It will first lead you through a field in which sheep may graze contentedly, then to a track through another field that bears to the left. Once reaching the boundary of this field, just keep going up (and up and up), smiling at those on their way down as you do so, as a powerful comradely spirit exists on this walk, between those who have conquered the hill and those who are about to.

The stiles on this track are created from massive stone blocks, but as

> *Pythius says*
>
> I rather enjoy showing off on a hill walk. This really annoys Helen, for while she is struggling with the climb, I run backwards and forwards showing what I am made of, and I don't slip as she does when the going gets rather muddy. That said, I admit it was good to find a drink of water waiting for me at the café once we reached the top.

they all have dog-friendly planks beside the stones that can be pulled up to reveal a dog-sized hole, this is not a problem.

You will pass through several fields where sheep graze, so obviously it is important to keep the dog on the lead if you spot them. You will eventually get to a steep bit where steps have been cut from the earth to aid walkers. Unfortunately, a hand rail has only been fitted for half the steps; walkers struggling with the climb could find this section difficult. One thing is certain though – you will not get lost. Way-markers are there in abundance on every stile and post – besides, so many people and their dogs walk this way it is just a matter of following the leader until you reach the top. There's only one real hazard and that is the mud which creates a rather slippery path that should be walked with care on a rainy day, particularly on the way down.

At the top, you can use the little dog-friendly restaurant besides the car park for refreshments, or unpack your picnic basket and make use of the tables set out for this purpose.

Of course you could drive to the top of the hill, park your car and picnic without the effort of walking to the top – but this is cheating and would deprive your dog of a thrilling walk.

Morris and Brown at the Tower

This restaurant situated next to the car park on the top of the hill caters for walkers and their dogs. A sign saying that dogs are welcome inside the café sets the scene, and they really are welcome! Fresh water is always available for canine visitors who are allowed to place their paws under any table they wish.

The food, served during the summer months until 3.30 pm, offers most things a walker could ask for, including hot soups, freshly made sandwiches, salads and an extensive assortment of hot meals.

The staff are really friendly and particularly helpful when you give your order, and prices are reasonable. It's just a shame it is not open during winter months when a hot meal would be really appreciated.

Burford:
Cotswold Wildlife Park
The Royal Oak

When our car turns off the A361 and into the gates of the Cotswold Wildlife Park, Burford, Pythius shows distinct signs of excitement. His ears go up, his tail wags and he starts to prepare to get out. Keeping him calm at this stage, when he is quivering with anticipation, is difficult. Despite having to be kept on a lead throughout his visit, it rates as one of his favourite places. Indeed he gets as excited as the children who often come with us.

It's not commonly known that dogs are allowed into the park; most of my friends are quite surprised to discover canines are welcome to join the family.

By allowing dogs into the park, a happy family day out is guaranteed, and be assured dogs really do love investigating all those strange animal smells and pressing their nose against the glass barriers to get a proper look at the inhabitants staring through the bars of their cages. It's the big cats that mesmerize Pythius, particularly the lions, who lie in a somnolent pose beside the barriers or parade proudly around their enclosure, stopping now and again to sniff the air and gaze at the visitors. As there is a considerable distance between these beautiful beasts and the glass barrier, there is no chance that a dangerous confrontation will ensue. In fact, all enclosures are secure in this 160-acre well-tended, landscaped parkland.

Dogs are even allowed to travel on the little train that weaves its way through the park, past the camels with their dark brown fur coats that fall in shaggy pieces from their skin, past the two giraffes who arrived to mark the park's 40th anniversary, the white rhino grazing peacefully and alongside the giant tortoises which amble around their enclosure. The tortoises fascinate Pythius. These massive beasts – the males weighing in at 250 kg – raise their heads when Pythius presses his nose against the fence around their enclosure. He in turn wags his tail after giving the tortoise a good sniff. It is such fun to watch.

He is delighted by the penguins too, and obviously the meerkats standing on guard like sentries always catch his eye.

Curator Jamie Craig walks round the park in the evening with his black labrador to check the animals as they prepare for sleep. He says it's the highlight of their day for them both as they walk from cage to cage, his dog sniffing all the delicious smells he encounters. Jamie says that historically dogs have always been allowed in the park, and speaks about 'Scruffs', the dog show that they organised for Comic Relief, which proved so successful they will probably hold it again.

He explains that obviously dogs must be kept on their leads during their visit to the park as there are some areas, such as the refurbished enclosure where the Humboldt penguins live, that have relatively low walls which keep the penguins in, but could be leapt by an energetic dog. The meerkats are in a similar enclosure.

Founded by John Heyworth in 1970, the wildlife park evolved from a small, innovative enterprise intended to revive the dilapidated manor house in the centre of the park. Since then it has been totally transformed and rates as one of the most beautiful and spacious wildlife parks in the country. It's good to know that dogs are welcome.

To find out more about the park, the 250 species of animals, insects

Pythius says:

The first time I was taken to the Cotswold Wildlife Park I was gobsmacked. Until that visit the only animals I was familiar with were domestic cats and the occasional dog I pass in the street. It was the animals' strange smells that mesmerized me so. Never had I smelt lion, camel or monkey before – it was all very puzzling. I am used to their smells now and have come to enjoy them. And the little train – well, that is amazing. How I love rattling through the animal enclosures, with the driver sounding his bell as we go. Every dog should experience this little train and enjoy what I enjoy. Helen has to pay a small fee for her ticket, but I get to go free!

and birds that live there and the special events organised for each year, go to its website: www.cotswoldwildlifepark.co.uk

There is a bustling little café on the premises, and tables placed close by where visitors can eat should they wish. The prices are reasonable and the food is good, but it is not licensed.

The Royal Oak, Burford

If you want to enjoy a glass of beer with your lunch you will have to travel to Burford, three miles away, and visit the Royal Oak in Witney Street, set just off the main High Street close to the town's little car park. It's a delightful old pub so dog-friendly that dogs are allowed in all areas, not just the bar. Pythius loves visiting this delightful pub and curling up on the polished flagstone floors, while we enjoy lunch.

The food here is reasonably priced and offers a fine choice of home cooked dishes and fine ales, and what's more food is served throughout the day until late in the evening. Where possible ingredients are sourced locally and cooked to order, which is an extra bonus.

While you enjoy your visit to this pub you can ponder on J. B. Priestley's comments about this charming market town and wonder if Burford is still as 'self-conscious' as he declared it was when traveling through the Cotswolds during his English Journey in the autumn of 1933.

Chedworth Roman Villa

The Seven Tuns

Three mile circular walk

Roman villas are found in abundance all over the Cotswolds, but none is as impressive as the magnificent villa at Chedworth, nestled among woodland at the top of a hill overlooking the idyllic little village of Chedworth. You will find it seven miles north of Cirencester: take a left-hand turn when travelling the A429 towards Stow-on-the-Wold. This will take you to Chedworth village or the villa.

In 2011 the villa underwent a £3 million transformation to help conserve and improve the property, thanks to Heritage Lottery Fund support. This has opened the site up nicely. Its superb collection of mosaics are now on full view and a splendid educational centre has been added to the site, which is in the safe hands of the National Trust.

Unfortunately only support dogs are permitted into the villa's visitors' area, but dogs are allowed to sit within an outside decking area where their masters can enjoy refreshments from the café. A drinking bowl for dogs is always provided.

As the surrounding woodlands in which the villa stands offer visitors a chance to walk some really lovely unspoiled wooded areas, it is somewhere I visit frequently. My friends and I get over the villa's dog ban by taking it in turns to explore the villa, while Pythius remains on the decking area, until his big moment when the walk can begin.

During one visit, Uncle John and I were amused to discover a floor tile in the villa bearing the imprint of a dog's footprint. No doubt it was created by a dog running over the tile as it dried in the sun. This suggests that dogs were allowed to wander the site once!

Car parking can be difficult for although there is a small car park to the left of the entrance, on a busy day drivers have to park on the verges of the small road leading to the villa. Don't let that put you off; this is one Cotswold site that should not be missed if you want to discover how life was in 4th-century Roman Britain. Arrive early in the morning in spring before the holiday season gets underway and before the villa gets too crowded, and parking near the villa is not a problem.

The pub

Two things will probably happen when you open the main door of the Seven Tuns pub, Chedworth and walk inside. The first will be an overwhelming feeling that you are stepping back in time, the second is that you will be met by such a sincere greeting you will know you have arrived at a special place and are welcome. It is indeed a very magical place, named (it is said) by the seven chimneys that once graced its roof.

Dating back to 1610, this unspoiled treasure offers everything you have dreamed of, if you get your kicks from visiting a real pub that pulsates with history. Just lifting the ancient latch to open the front door is an experience.

The food is great, freshly cooked and served in generous portions and the beer is varied. This is a pub we visit often, if only to remind ourselves that pubs like this really do exist. Of course Pythius is welcome, but when he asks for water, he is invited to take it from the bowl placed on the opposite side of the road, next to a natural spring that tumbles through the wall. As this water is cool and crisp he often drinks more than he should.

The Seven Tuns is but a couple of miles drive from the Roman villa, in the village of Chedworth. You will find signposts to Chedworth close to the villa.

The walk from the villa

If you walk in spring you will encounter an abundance of wild flowers including primroses, bluebells and cowslips in large clusters. Indeed this walk opens up a perfect microcosm of the Cotswold hills as it incorporates the beauty of the Coln Valley, ancient woodlands, well-grazed meadows and a picture box village that lies besides a tributary of the river Coln, which is but a rippling stream at this point.

On leaving the villa, walk a few yards down the road, taking the first right-hand turning into a minor road, providing you with panoramic views of grazing sheep on the right-hand side and woodland on the left.

You will soon come to a small road on the right; ignore that and continue for a short distance more until you come to some stone steps on the right which lead to Chedworth Wood and the real start to a superb walk through the most picturesque woodland. It's uphill to begin with, but it soon levels out, revealing wild flowers and a grassy carpet that stretches out between the trees. Well placed way-markers will guide you until you reach a large field with a well defined footpath cut into the soil. This will lead you to a gate and another minor road. Turn right having passed through the gate (having put the dog on the lead) and walk this road until you come to a right-hand turn which is way-marked the Monarch's Way. This takes you along a fenced path and past the most somnolent black-faced sheep you may ever meet – they certainly seemed quite unperturbed when we stopped to photograph them before walking on. You may well pass a large herd of cows next, who are kept within their territory by an electric fence. As you walk you will see the village of Chedworth coming into view in the valley below. It is all very idyllic and picturesque.

This path takes you to a large sweeping path that leads back into the woods and eventually two footpath signs, one pointing one way and one the other. Take the right-hand path, and amble through the woods under an old red-brick railway bridge and back to the Roman villa.

Pythius says:

I don't know how Helen manages to come up with such splendid walks – pubs too. I admit that staying outside the villa on the decking area and not being allowed in is tedious, but knowing that a walk follows makes it all worthwhile. Besides, Helen seems to enjoy visiting the villa so much, how could I spoil her fun with a sulk? Impossible.

Cranham

The Black Horse

Gustav Holst

Two-mile circular walk through Buckholt Wood

Perhaps we should have waited until the snow had fallen before taking this walk. Then, as we ambled through Buckholt Wood, singing our enthusiastic rendition of Christina Rossetti's Christmas poem *In the Bleak Midwinter* to which Gustav Holst supplied the melody, our choice of music would have would have been far more appropriate.

We were walking the woods on a sunny day in the middle of summer, but recent rains had rendered the earth slippery and to Pythius's delight had also filled the little stream that twists and turns through the woods. He had a great time darting in and out of the stream as we walked in the footsteps of Gustav Holst, one of the country's greatest composers – singing as we went.

We enjoyed lunch at the Black Horse in Cranham which stands opposite Midwinter Cottage, where Holst stayed in 1904. It was during this period that he set Christina Rossetti's poem to music. It seemed appropriate to sing it whilst we walked through one of the woods he loved so much – besides neither of us could remember enough of The Planets suite to hum other pieces he had composed!

The Black Horse is a delightful, rustic, unspoiled and friendly Cotswold stone pub which stands at the top of a steep narrow lane. The car park is further up the lane. As there are two resident pub dogs, Pythius was certainly made welcome.

Whilst there is no proof that Holst actually visited the pub, it would

be good to imagine him penning the tune in Cranham while enjoying a pint in the pub opposite the house in which he was living at the time.

The main bar features a huge cast-iron fireplace

and a red quarry-tiled floor, while chunky wooden chairs and tables add their special touch. A choice of three real ales on tap turns it into a true pub.

Having walked the woods for some considerable time, we were ready for a couple of hot toasted sandwiches from the pub's menu, which were filled with hand-cut home-cooked ham and beautifully served with a suitable garnish. Prices for both food and drink are modest and nothing about the décor suggests that this is a tourist destination, though obviously now the Holst Way has been opened, it will almost certainly attract more walkers.

The walk

We left our car in the car park at the top of the hill, and walked from the pub, past Midwinter Cottage on the left, to the main road that winds through Cranham. On turning right having crossed the road, we spotted the footpath way-sign which would guide us through Buckholt Wood. It's a dark, almost foreboding sort of wood, and yes I did expect little creatures, hobgoblins perhaps, or little green men from one of the planets, to jump out in front of us. I think that is why Uncle John and I began singing, and why Pythius stuck to playing in the stream which wound its way through the woods. After about 70 yards the path twists and divides – we took the right-hand branch, which led us away from the official route.

As Holst is known to have roamed these woods frequently and as we were looking for a short circular route, it didn't seem to matter if we strayed off the official path. We were confident that he would have occasionally walked this way too. If you take the official route that has been devised for us by Brian Carvell you will spot yellow directional arrows marked on the trees to guide you forward and eventually to the Air Balloon public house at the bottom of Crickley Hill on the A417 roundabout. Sadly dogs are not allowed inside this Greene King pub, though they are welcome to sit outside in the garden with their masters.

Pythius says

I guess listening to Helen and Uncle John singing Christmas carols is OK if they just sing one or two and then stop. Trouble with Helen is that she never knows when to stop. On and on they went, repeating the same tune over and over, driving me barking mad and frightening all the birds in the woods. I am sure that the nice composer chap who walked this way did so in silence. Besides, who wants to sing of snow when the sun is shining?

The pub was lovely, nice cool floor to lie on, nice young woman behind the bar to talk to while Helen and Uncle John were chomping through their lunch.

As the woods are criss-crossed with numerous footpaths, I guess it might be quite easy to get lost, though we didn't. Perhaps that was because we took the walk at a gentle pace, allowing Holst's music to guide us on our way. Having circumnavigated the woods we ambled back to the pub.

The Gustav Holst Way

This 35-mile way takes the walker from Cranham to Wyck Rissington, via Cheltenham and Bourton, all places known to Holst. This route opened officially in 2011, having been devised by Brian Carvell, one-time Trustee of the Holst Birthplace Museum, and set up by a group of volunteers. It can be walked either way. It was created to encourage walkers to become familiar with Holst's love of the Cotswolds and his many associations with this part of England. We walked just a couple of miles, but how far you go is up to you. If you follow the first part of the Gustav Holst Way, which begins at Cranham Church where Holst's mother used to play the harmonium, this section is just under 6 miles.

For further information and an online guide to The Gustav Holst Way go to www.holstmuseum.org.uk

You will find the museum, which is the Regency house where Holst was born in 1874, at 4 Clarence Road, Cheltenham GL52 2AY (phone 01242 524846). It is open from 10am to 4pm, but closed from mid-December to early February.

Down Ampney
The Old Spotted Cow, Marston Meysey

Ralph Vaughan Williams

Gentle two-mile walk round the village walking in the composer's footsteps

There are four Ampneys – Down Ampney, Ampney St Peter, Ampney and Ampney Crucis, all a few miles from each other close to the border between Gloucestershire and Wiltshire and located close to the Cotswold Water Park, five miles south-east of Cirencester.

We chose Down Ampney, birthplace of Ralph Vaughan Williams (1872–1958), one of England's greatest composers. His *The Lark Ascending* is one of the most popular works in the classical repertoire. As son of the Reverend Arthur Vaughan Williams, he lived in the village of Down Ampney for three years, moving with his family to Dorking after his father's death. The Old Vicarage is now a private house, but there's an excellent little exhibition detailing the main areas of his life in All Saints Church on the outskirts of the village. This impressive little church is a Grade I listed building originally built by the Knights Templar and consecrated in 1265. Its remoteness from the centre of the village is due largely to the Black Death which hit this area badly, causing survivors to settle elsewhere.

The walk

It's worth starting your walk from the church, having parked your car just off the road close to the lych gate. All the church kneelers have been hand worked with scenes that depict the village and its inhabitants, so look out for the one bearing Vaughan Williams' name. While you are there, having checked out the small exhibition, do spend a moment or two admiring the Arnhem Memorial window and the altar frontal depicting past and present elements in the village.

On leaving the church turn right and away from the village. You will spot an old metal kissing gate and a way sign beside the church wall, but this narrow path is rather overgrown, so it is advisable to take to the small tree-lined road instead which appears to run parallel to the footpath.

Before you begin walking, note the large map opposite the lych gate. It is one of several maps placed in prominent positions round the village to enable walkers to enjoy the many footpaths that encircle Down Ampney.

Walk the lane for about a quarter of a mile, until you come to a gate, turn sharply left and follow the track that will take you first past a farmhouse and a metal gate. You will also notice a sign at this point saying 'Dogs on Leads' – this was the only place where we encountered this request, and assumed therefore it was only applicable to the small area before the gate and by the farm house. The green lane ahead continues in a straight line for just under half a mile, perhaps less, taking the walker over two small stone bridges which straddle the bed of a small stream.

Pythius rushed towards the bridge with enthusiasm only to discover there was no water. Dried up river beds are something we encounter all too often these days.

On reaching a right-hand turn linking with another footpath in the direction of Down Ampney, we first walked on for a few yards, to admire a cluster of buildings and church tower half hidden by the trees, just a short distance away. It is the village of Latton, an archetypal sight worth taking the time to enjoy.

Return to the footpath on the right that you passed as this will take you back to the village. It carries on for about half a mile until you reach the main road, and passes through tree-lined areas and open country. Secure the dog's lead, turn right on reaching the road and towards a sign informing visitors they are entering Ralph Vaughan Williams' birthplace. Now it's a matter of following the road as it curves to the right and continues back towards the church. Very few cars travel this way, so we released Pythius at this point.

The Old Spotted Cow, Marston Meysey

A two-mile trip in the car brings you to this superb country pub three miles east of Cricklade and not far from RAF Fairford. If you are feeling energetic you could walk there.

I love this 200-year old pub, set back from The Street that passes through Marston Meysey. This pub not only serves great food and well-kept beer, it treats all its customers

as if they are special, and that includes the four-legged variety. Pythius was offered a couple of bone-shaped biscuits as soon as he entered and more when we were served our meal. His bowl of water arrived promptly – even before we had been served our beer which was Sheep Dip, a great real ale from the Wiltshire brewery Plain Ales.

If you hadn't noticed the name of the pub on entering, the pictures that adorn its walls leave you in no doubt! Paintings, sketches and sculptures of spotted cows are everywhere. So many spotted cows that I wondered why there were none grazing the large area of grass outside too.

This is one of those pubs where the service is impeccable, the staff are not just courteous and helpful, but appear to be working all-out to offer customers a real hospitality experience. On the day we arrived, they seemed particularly concerned that their customers were having a good time. And we were. How could it be otherwise? This is a superb country pub set in a tranquil country location just outside the village of Marston Meysey. It deserves to be busy.

Pythius says

Not sure I go much on visiting old churches. I find that they often smell musty and Helen spends far too long lingering as she inspects everything. Then out comes the camera and she walks around all over again, clicking the shutter as if she is on an important mission.

The walk would have been really good if there had been water flowing under the bridge. No water, just weeds and a few clusters of watercress. No fields to run round either, and far too many roads for my liking, but it was a pretty village and I liked the pub, where I was treated with great kindness. I just wish that Helen and Uncle John hadn't kept humming that tune about a lark flying in the sky above them. It was autumn, and I certainly didn't see any larks.

Ducklington
The Bell

Mollie Harris

A two-mile river walk

Although broadcaster and writer Mollie Harris spent much of her adult life in the village of Eynsham, her childhood home was Ducklington, near Witney.

It was a childhood she describes in glorious detail in her first book, *A Kind of Magic*, published in 1969. Her sense of wonder at all that affected her daily life in Ducklington – searching for the first wild flowers of the season, sliding on a frozen pond at night in the crisp frosty air and the joy of home-made jam boiling on the open fire – provides an insight into the way this remarkable woman took joy in small things that coloured her life. Her many radio broadcasts were both informative and amusing, but she is best known for playing Martha in the BBC Radio 4's long-running series *The Archers*.

She opens her first book by stating that the days of her childhood seemed to have a kind of magic about them. This magic is scattered throughout all her published works and certainly wove its way through everything she undertook, be it broadcasting or brewing up large jars of home-made country wine. Those who assumed her wine was just a fruity lemonade and drank it as such, often discovered their legs giving way when they tried to get up from their chair.

Ducklington stands one mile south of Witney and closed to the west bank of the River Windrush. Its name is thought to originate from the central duck pond close to the church and the Bell Inn, where ducks and their ducklings have lived for centuries. Sadly, the pond water has now drained; all you can see is an indentation in the earth where the pond used to be, now overgrown with weeds. Not a duck in sight. The disturbing thing is that this has happened since our first book *Paws Under the Table* where I commented on the moment Pythius nearly pulled me into the pond when he spotted the ducks and rushed after them with me clutching desperately onto his lead.

This ancient village, which dates back to Saxon times, is now famous for the rare fritillary flowers that flourish in a meadow just outside the village, reached along the lane behind the church. Once a year the residents hold a Fritillary Day to celebrate this beautiful flower. Visitors are permitted to walk the field and admire this delicate bloom. Even Pythius is allowed into the field, which pleases him greatly.

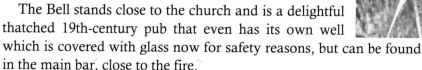

The Bell stands close to the church and is a delightful thatched 19th-century pub that even has its own well which is covered with glass now for safety reasons, but can be found in the main bar, close to the fire.

We love this pub as it is so cosy and dogs are welcomed in the main bar area where the locals prop up the bar and put the world to rights. Delicious home-cooked food at a reasonable price is served in the bar area on rustic scrubbed tables by friendly professional staff who always make us feel at home. This is one pub where the chips are hand cut and taste scrumptious – all crispy on the outside and soft and floury on the inside. Order a sandwich and you get a real meal as it comes with an attractive small wire container of these chips and a generous salad garnish. Pythius adores coming here, and so do we because the beer is as good as the company.

The walk

Turning left out of the pub and pass the Old School House where Mollie went to school. It's a domestic dwelling now. In Mollie's days it accommodated children from outlying villages and hamlets as well as the youngsters from Ducklington. Many would walk two or three miles

Pythius says

I love the big log fire in the Bell that dances with heat during the cold weather. The people who run this pub are kind and seem to love Border collies – so do the customers, many of whom appear to be farmers.

The walk beside the river is wonderful as it is river, river and river all the way, though I am not allowed to leap in and splash about during the spring when water birds are nesting.

I do laugh when the girls stride out during a rainy period as they do frequently on this walk. They are optimists and assume the walk will be pass-able all the way, then discover to their horror that their boots are getting stuck in slurping mud that covers both boots and the edges of their trousers. They are not happy bunnies when this happens. Me? Oh, I am fine. I just run through the mud and have a wonderful time as my black and white fur grad-ually turns a sticky chocolate brown.

over muddy fields to get there, clutching their lunch which, like Mollie's, might have consisted of hunks of bread and dripping or lumps of bread pudding. They would also take a screw of paper holding a spoonful of sugar and cocoa, to be transformed into a midday hot drink when the teacher put the kettle on.

Pass the Old School House, turn left and take the road alongside the 12th-century St Bartholomew's Church, then walk the lane behind the church that leads to the Fritillary Field and other meadows. At the end of the lane you have a choice: either walk to the left and eventually reach the Witney Lake, where there is water in abundance and a great mile-long circular walk around the lake, or turn right and follow the Windrush Path that follows the river as it winds its way to Hardwick, Standlake and then Newbridge where the river meets the Thames.

No instructions are necessary for the second walk as the Windrush path is well marked and providing you keep the river on your right on the way out, there is nothing else you need to know, except that during wet winter periods it can be very muddy. Walk to Hardwick and you will have walked about two miles. I realise it is not a circular walk and you have to return the way you came when you are ready, but be assured, it is a lovely walk that takes you past fields of curious sheep who rush to greet visitors and large lakes created from disused quarries.

Given that Mollie spent much of her childhood exploring the meadows surrounding her village, as well as the river, you will certainly be walking the area she loved.

Dursley, Stinchcombe Hill
The Old Spot Inn

Cotswold Way and Korea Friendship Trail

Three-and-a-half-mile circular walk

By exploring the Cotswold Way's circular walk around the top of Stinchcombe Hill, Gloucestershire, you will be walking the world's first Friendship Trail. Stinchcombe Hill is part of the Cotswold Edge, set on the southern escarpment above the Severn valley. It offers superb views to the Forest of Dean, the Black Mountains, the Malvern Hills, the Bristol Channel and North Devon, and forms a magnificent back-drop to the market town of Dursley where this glorious walk begins.

The twinning of a walk along the Cotswold Way, with a similar walk on the Jeju Island, off the southwest coast of Korea, is an exciting new initiative that came about as a result of the World Trails conference on Jeju Island, attended by representatives of the Cotswold Way.

Essentially, the idea is similar to the twin town concept which enables people from two similar places, but in different parts of the world, to team up with each other. It's hoped that this idea will soon spread across the globe.

The trail is marked as both the Cotswold Way and with signs of the Jeju Olle, which is known as the Ganse and shaped like the Jeju pony, which appears on the Korean trail. The word Ganse translates as 'lazy bones' and for good reason as both trails wind their way through breathtakingly

beautiful terrains which should be absorbed at a pace slow enough to embrace all before you and allow time to fully appreciate the landscape that spreads out towards the horizon.

The pub

The Old Spot Inn, which stands opposite Dursley's free public car park and only two minutes walk from the beginning of the Korea Friendship Trail, is known as 'A pub of a thousand locals' and is also described as one of Gloucestershire's 'must-visits'. You know why the moment you open the front door and enter this busy buzzing little place. The staff here are well aware of the meaning of the word hospitality. Never have we encountered so many happy smiles and sparkling eyes. It's one of those traditional boozers that offers just that little bit extra and yes, dogs are very welcome. Pythius was patted on the head by staff passing our table several times and, as we had not found rivers during our walk, was eager to taste the water they presented to him.

The choice of real ales is terrific and includes the Original Butcombe Bitter and even Penny Black Porter, a smooth full-bodied porter brewed by the Gloucestershire brewery Wickwar. The Old Spot, which is decorated throughout with brewery memorabilia, tends to its beers so well it was voted the Best Cask Ales Pub of 2011 at the Great British Beer Awards.

The food is great too. We chose hot beef sandwiches but a reasonably priced menu also offers a fine choice of hot meals. This hundred-year-old pub definitely deserves all the accolades it receives.

The walk

On leaving the pub, turn left and walk to where May Lane meets Hill Road, which is signposted with way-markers for both the Cotswold Way and the Korea Friendship Trail. This is a steep trail that will take you up a 200-yard trek, before a sharp bend and a kissing gate that leads to a wooded area and then a golf clubhouse at the top of Stinchcombe Hill. As this path is quite steep and perhaps a little too arduous for those who seek a more gentle terrain, you can avoid this section by driving along the B4060 to a public car park at the top of the hill and begin your walk from there.

On reaching the top of the hill, either by driving or walking, you will notice signs to the Cotswold Way at the edge of the public car park, offering two alternatives, left or right. Start your walk by taking the path on the right-hand side, ignoring the path straight through the woods, then begin following this well-marked way in a clockwise direction. Soon you will emerge from a stand of trees and be facing one of the most spectacular view points of the whole walk. A bench is strategically positioned here to enable you to soak up this view before going on.

A stone cabin about half a mile on has been erected to provide shelter during inclement weather conditions. The cabin also offers great views of the River Severn.

There's not much else you need to know about the route, which if followed will return you to the place where you first started, having first guided you past some of the most spectacular views in the Cotswolds.

Unfortunately there is a slight downside to this walk – it circum-navigates a 19-hole golf course. In places the green and fairway are but a few yards from the track you will be taking. During our visit Uncle John, Pythius and I stopped to admire the view when suddenly out of nowhere a golf ball flew past our heads at a really terrifying speed. It missed us by just a few inches. Walkers on footpaths and bridleways have the right of way as the top of the hill was given to the public by Sir Stanley Tubbs and is registered as common land. However, much of this land is managed by Stinchcombe Hill Golf Club which has had a 99-year lease on the site since 1929. Sadly disputes between walkers and golfers go back to the 1930s.

Pythius says:

What a walk! What amazing views. I don't think Helen and Uncle John believe I can admire views, but I can. It does my spirit good to see all that land laid out before me waiting to be explored. Views remind me that the world is a wonderful place and that there is so much out there I haven't yet travelled. I admit to being slightly alarmed when that golf ball flew over our heads, but fortunately it went on to hit a tree, then rolled down the dip out of sight and into the foliage below.

Enstone

The Crown, Church Enstone

Walking the footsteps of farm worker Mont Abbott

To capture the true character of farm worker Mont Abbott, who spent his life in the Enstone area, perhaps I should write about him using an Oxfordshire country accent. But I doubt I could capture the essence of the man as Sheila Stewart has in her atmospheric little book *Lifting the Latch*, which describes his life on the land as carter and shepherd (1902–1989). A blue plaque was placed on the cottage in which he lived out the later years of his life in the nearby hamlet of Fulwell – such is the importance of his place in a rural Cotswold society which celebrates him still.

Mont always kept two sheep dogs, the training of the young one overlapping from the old, though he would never let the young ones follow the experienced dog for too long, in case they lost their initiative. His favourite dogs were old Ted and young Glen, who followed the old dog's footsteps, and turned out to be a topping dog. I doubt there is a field in the Enstone area that Mont and his dogs did not work at some time or other.

Pythius comes from farming stock and I often wonder what kind of working dog he would have made if I hadn't taken him to be my companion. His eyes still light up and his tail twitches when he spots a field of sheep, and he turns left or right on command, so perhaps he would have been a topping sheep dog too if I had given him a chance, rather than teaching him to write?

The Crown

Pythius and I love visiting the Crown. It is one of those warm friendly 17th-century pubs built in honey-coloured Cotswold stone, that heats the bar area with a splendid crackling open fire during the winter. The staff always makes us feel at home when we call. Mont lifted the latch of the Crown when he was just a boy. Sadly the main door he used has been replaced – you open the new one by twisting a door knob now, but the ancient metal latch he also lifted when entering St Kenelm's Church nearby remains firmly in place.

Dogs are always welcomed in the Crown, though I doubt Mont would have been accompanied by his beloved sheep dogs when he entered; they were working dogs not companions. We often arrive with three dogs walking in beside us: Pythius, Polly-dog and Auntie Kate's delightful springer spaniel puppy called Alfie.

A large bowl of water outside the Crown's main door signifies canines are welcome, and another inside beside the fire says the same.

The food is scrumptious and the choice of dishes exciting. Old Mont would no doubt be thrilled to discover his village pub still uses local game and other seasonal products to create its dishes. He would have certainly approved of the dish of bubble and squeak, served with slices of crispy bacon and a fresh local egg, for which the Crown is so well known. An old fashioned dish it may be, but it is one of the most popular items on the menu.

Locally brewed real ales such as Hook Norton's Old Hooky are always available. Old Hooky is one of the main ingredients in their much prized Steak and Hooky pie that comes with proper shortcrust pastry.

The walk

Walking in Mont's footsteps is easy once you reach Enstone; apart from that first journey when he and his family left Oxford to live in this area in a horse-drawn removal van at the age of three, he never lived anywhere else. He says he lived near Neat Enstone, Church Enstone and Cleveley, all but a stone's throw from each other, and therefore (to use Mont's terminology), they all be 'our Enstone'. So to walk the pastures he worked, just follow the nearest way-sign and go from there. The way between the pub and the church takes you down a little lane beside the churchyard, which in turn takes you to the first of a series of meadows that stretch into the far distance and eventually reach Heythrop Park. The views along this well-defined path are as they were in Mont's day, and the wild flowers that flourish in the first meadow a reminder that some areas in the Oxfordshire Cotswolds remain unspoiled. We usually walk a long mile when taking this route, then turn and come back the way we came.

To view Mont's cottage in Fulwell and the blue plaque, begin your walk in the centre of Enstone, crossing the busy A44 that runs through the village – taking care as this road is seldom without traffic. Look for Cox's Lane on the left and follow it for about a quarter of a mile, until you pass the village sports ground and meet up with the B4022. Once again, cross this road with care, taking the small road opposite which passes the ancient Hoar Stone burial chamber and on to the little hamlet of Fulwell. The Hoar Stone is on the right, just a few yards down the road, but is so heavily shrouded with dense foliage you could easily pass it unnoticed.

Fulwell comprises just a few small estate cottages, one of which bears the blue plaque. Do stop and admire it for a moment and soak

> ### *Pythius says*
>
> Helen often worries about turning me into a companion dog when I could have been out in the field with someone like Mont herding in the sheep. She needn't worry. I have a great life looking after her and the food she serves is fantastic, far better, I am sure, than anything a working sheep dog would get. Besides, I get to run free in meadows and fields all over the Cotswolds without having to bother to collect sheep as I go.
>
> Love the pub, this is where I come with Polly-dog and Kate when we meet up for a walk and lunch. She has got a new puppy now, so he comes too. Actually he is a dear little chap, and like Mont's dogs he watches what Polly and I do and does the same. It certainly didn't take him long to learn how to curl up in front of the log fire.

up the atmosphere such a lovely little cottage evokes. Now take the next footpath on the left-hand side which passes through a gate and a large field which usually has cattle grazing there. Just keep to the field edge on the right-hand side and take no notice of the cattle; these gentle creatures are used to walkers invading their territory. When the path divides, take the left-hand path which leads uphill to the A44. Once again, cross with care as traffic speeds along this road at a tremendous rate. Once safely across, you can enjoy walking through an atmospheric wooded area in which your dog can run free.

This finally opens out onto a grass track and well-worn path that leads to a few cottages over a tarmac road and a narrow lane that eventually opens out into another tarmac road. You have now reached the hamlet of Cleveley. Take the footpath directly opposite, which runs to the left of the short terrace of cottages downhill to a track past a large pond (some might call it a lake). You see an attractive house ahead. Bypassing the house and keeping to the path that bears left, you can now enjoy walking a lovely country lane that Mont would have undoubtedly known well. This will eventually take you to the B4022. Cross the road, and take the charmingly named (although not signposted) Cling Clang Lane straight ahead, turning left when it meets another road at the far end. Now you should spot the church tower in the near distance, so walk on just a little further keeping that in sight as the church and pub only stand a little way from each other, then turn right down a small unnamed road to the pub, where a delicious lunch and a cool drinks awaits.

Farmcote
Hailes Abbey, Farmcote Herbs and Chilli Pepper Farm

Two-mile walk

Auntie Caroline, Pythius and I came across the Farmcote Herbs and Chilli Pepper Farm quite unexpectedly, while walking an uphill bridle-path and the Cotswold Way that links the ruins of Hailes Abbey with the little hamlet of Farmcote. It undoubtedly rates as one of the most beautiful parts of the Cotswolds.

Suddenly there it was at the top of the hill – a small nursery specialising in herbs and chilli peppers, with an outlook towards the Malvern Hills and the Black Mountains of Wales. The hard-working couple, Tim Hand and Jane Eayrs, have turned their plot of land into a fertile little place that is overflowing with unusual plants. Had we not arrived on foot, Caroline and I would have undoubtedly left armed with a multitude of hand-reared plants. Next time perhaps we will drive to the nursery then walk down hill to Hailes Abbey, which would enable us to fill the car with our purchases, as there are more than 200 different chilli plants of all marvellous shapes and sizes to choose from. Of

course, that would only work if we ate our picnic at the top of the hill rather than in the ruins of Hailes Abbey. But given the spectacular views at the top of the hill, this would not be a hardship.

Yes – this is a picnic walk; there are pubs in nearby Winchcombe, known as the Cotswold Walking Centre, but now and again, if the weather is being kind to us, Caroline and I pack a picnic when walking. We particularly enjoy sitting in what was once the kitchen area of the atmospheric abbey ruins munching on our sandwiches

and raising our glasses to the beauty of the Cotswolds. After exploring the ruins, enjoying all those ancient scents, Pythius usually potters back and sits beside us waiting patiently for crumbs to fall from our picnic table.

Farmcote consists of just two farms, six houses and a very pretty little Saxon church, with the Cotswold Way running down to Hailes Abbey. As there is a Cotswold gem at each end of the walk, this little track through a wooded area makes for a delightful walk. And with vistas of surrounding countryside opening up now and again between the trees, this walk is a real joy for although it is uphill all the way to Farmcote, it is not so steep as to make things arduous.

Hailes Abbey, which is now a National Trust property, occupies a secluded position near the foot of a westward-facing slope of the Cotswolds, two miles north-east of Winchcombe and off the B4632. The abbey was founded by Richard, Earl of Cornwall, who vowed to establish a religious house if he was saved when at danger whilst at sea in 1242, as he was. In 1245, his brother King Henry III gave him the manor of Hailes so that he could keep this pledge. Once it was estab-

> **Pythius says**
>
> I love the abbey ruins – the smells are simply fantastic. I can feel its history creeping into my paws and up into my body. All very exciting actually, though the girls seem more interested in the old stones and their picnic than the earth on which we walk.

lished, Richard's son Edmund presented the Cistercian monks of Hailes Abbey with a phial said to contain he blood of Christ. Until the Dissolution, Hailes Abbey became a magnet for pilgrims.

Today modern pilgrims make their way there to soak up the mystic atmosphere generated by these ancient ruins, which thanks to the National Trust are all marked so that it is easy to identify each of the areas still exposed to the elements. A small museum is attached, that is also well worth visiting. As it is a National Trust property there are modest entry charges, but be assured they are worth it, particularly if you have brought a picnic.

The walk

On leaving Hailes Abbey, turn left and make your way past the fruit farm where an abundance of fantastic freshly harvested fruits and vegetables are available in season, and on down the small road for a short distance until you spot the way sign leading you to an uphill track taking you to Farmcote, under a mile away. The chilli farm is closed during the winter months, but the view, which looks particularly beautiful when frost decorates the trees, still makes this walk worthwhile. Should you wish, you can follow the Cotswold Way signs and extend the walk further, indeed you can go on to Winchcombe if you like.

Filkins

The Five Alls

Cotswold Woollen Weavers Heritage Centre

One-mile gentle amble around the village of Filkins

Sheep have grazed the Cotswold hills for more than 2,000 years, thanks to the Romans who are said to have brought them here. Their soft lustrous wool was the commodity that brought great wealth to the Cotswolds. Without their fleece there would be none of the great wool churches that dominate the local towns and stand as testament to the wealth of the medieval merchants who endowed them. Five hundred years ago it was thought that half the wealth of England rode on the back of the sheep, the finest wool coming from the Cotswolds.

Cotswold sheep are lovely creatures with dark but kindly eyes. The top of the head is covered with wool, not hair, and is distinguished by the fine tuft on the forehead. Their bodies are firm and solid to touch and well covered with thick set, long wool.

They call them the Lion of the Cotswold, a well-deserved title as they really are the most magnificent of sheep. Without sheep continually grazing the Cotswold fields and hills, the landscape would not look well-kept and tidy. They are the lawn-mowers that keep the landscape in order.

Until quite recently Cotswold wool was lumped in with other English lustre-wools and used mainly for carpets and industrial cloths. However, the Cotswold Woollen Weavers recognised its potential and revived its use in the early 1960s; it is now used to create beautiful fashionable garments and soft furnishings such as those created at the Cotswolds Woollen Weavers Heritage Centre, that stands a little way back from the main road that twists its way through the picturesque little village of Filkins. Here you can watch Cotswold wool being woven as it has been for centuries and take your time wandering through the extensive sales rooms where garments, hats and soft furnishings are on sale.

The Five Alls

This charming 18th-century pub with its flagstone floors, open fire and wooden ceiling is a delight. It is one of those hidden Cotswold gems that offers everything you expect and just a little bit more. Whilst dogs are not allowed in the stylish restaurant with its chunky wooden furniture, they are certainly welcome in the bar area. They are even offered a little dish of dog biscuits when their master's lunch is served, enabling everyone to eat together. Pythius liked that and chomped them down happily, while we stared with wonder at the beautifully presented dish of haddock and chips that was placed before us. It was so carefully arranged, with the chips served in a little newspaper cone, that it would have been easy to imagine we were dining in a five-star hotel, rather than a country pub. As the chips had been cooked in goose fat and were crisp and crunchy, they tasted fantastic and the fish succulent and juicy.

Customers are often puzzled by the name of this pub. Did the artist painting the pub sign get his letters muddled? Should it have been the 'Five Ales' rather than the Five Alls? After all, they do serve some very fine ale. No, look carefully at the sign and you will see it shows the devil in the middle, surrounded by a lawyer who pleads for all, a parson who prays for all, a soldier who fights for all, and a farmer who pays for all. It seems that it is the devil in the middle who governs all.

As the Five Alls is a Brakspear pub, Brakspear's Best Bitter and Oxford Gold are always on tap, which means that customers can enjoy a real ale brewed locally at the nearby market town of Witney, while savouring a meal cooked with local ingredients. This is a pub we take Pythius to often as the food is not just good, but reasonably priced and the atmosphere warm, friendly and comfortable.

The walk

This gentle amble takes you from The Five Alls to the Cotswolds Woollen Weavers Heritage Centre via a couple of meadows and a little lane. It once boasted a little stream too, but over the years the stream has dried up and is now just a dry dip in the field covered with weeds and watercress.

Pythius says

Why on earth do the girls love shopping so much? When they head for the heritage centre, I just know that one or other of them is going to come out of the showrooms clutching a carrier bag? Last time they were there, Helen looked for a hat to go with her walking jacket and Auntie Liz bought a posh woollen coat.

Once during the winter months, they contemplated asking if the centre would make me a little woollen jacket to keep out the rain during the winter months; a scary moment, particularly when the woman serving them began looking for her tape measure. Thank goodness they sensed my mood this time and bought themselves lovely woollen scarves instead.

The walk begins as you turn left out of the pub along the main road that travels through the village, past a magnificent yew hedge on the left, then past St Peter's Church and the war memorial. Next comes Rouse Lane on the left-hand side. The red pillar box marks the spot.

Walk down the lane, past the village shop on the left with its blue plaque dedicated to Sir Stafford Cripps, statesman and benefactor to the village, until you come to a stile which leads you to a rather muddy path through a coppice. During the spring this area is thick with wild snowdrops, such that it looks as if it has been snowing. They are a beautiful sight. You will eventually leave this path and enter a grassy field via a stile on the right-hand side. A well-worn path across a field marks the rest of the way, though we often walk Pythius round the entire field to extend his walk. The path eventually turns into another field on the right and the one-time stream which is no more, and then onto the Cotswold Wool Heritage Centre.

There is an exceptionally tall stone stile that leads to a lane and the main street back through the village. Instead of struggling to get over it we chose to let ourselves out via the centre's car park though a gate as even Pythius was concerned about the height of this stile when he first saw it.

Unfortunately dogs are not allowed into the centre, but as there are picnic tables outside, we usually buy steaming hot cups of tea from the café attached to the centre and drink them in the fresh air, taking it in turns to look after Pythius if we want to go inside and look around.

Finstock

The Plough Inn

T. S. Eliot

Two-mile circular walk which incorporates the church in which T. S. Eliot was baptised

When he was young, the poet T. S. Eliot visited churches to admire their beauty. In his later years it was the sense of peace, contemplation and spiritual refreshment they offered that drew him towards them. His visit to the Church of the Holy Trinity, Finstock in June 1927, however, was behind closed doors. At the age of 39, he was there to be baptised and received into the Church of England by his friend William Force Stead. For Eliot, this was a time of struggle and uncertainty, sandwiched between happier periods in his life, hence the creation of his poem Journey of the Magi, which is a part of Eliot's conversion story. It tells of him being ill at ease in the 'old dispensation' after his conversion and speaks of happiness during darker periods.

You will discover Holy Trinity Church on the edge of this charming little village sitting back from the B4022. As it has recently been refurbished it may not look exactly as it was when Eliot was baptised, but you will find it a joy to visit. Finstock is an attractive little village that overlooks the Evenlode Valley and lies in a clearing of the ancient royal hunting forest of Wychwood. You will find it two miles south of Charlbury off the Witney road.

The Plough Inn

The Plough is a delightful 17th-century thatched pub where Auntie Liz and I take Pythius when we want to treat ourselves to a really tasty meal and be spoiled by Joe and Martin who have run it for many years. If we get there early enough we can park ourselves besides a crackling fire in the small bar area, enjoying the comfort of large snuggly leather chairs. Otherwise we sit in the main bar area where we usually find ourselves enjoying animated conversations with other guests; such is the conviviality generated by our hosts.

Pythius really loves this pub as the boys always make a great fuss of him. They have their own dog now, a glorious golden Labrador named Bella who walks from table to table to check that everyone is happy. Pythius was rather apprehensive about her presence at first, but they are firm friends now and often sit together with their paws under our table waiting patiently for that wonderful moment when we accidentally allow something from our plates to drop to the floor. Actually it's a futile wait now as Joe and Martin have created a message on the blackboard which says PLEASE DO NOT FEED THE DOG, which is written in 12 different languages. Since they put that sign up, Bella has lost half a stone in weight!

The Plough Inn's menu celebrates local food in style which means that pheasant and other game birds are listed during the autumn and winter months and the summer menu makes much of fresh asparagus and strawberries. Their real ale selection includes local brews and has never failed us yet.

You will find the Plough in The Bottom, so named because it really is at the bottom of the hill. Although it attracts a great many tourists and walkers, it is also a community pub that offers villagers a place to meet up, talk and hold local events. There should be more community pubs like this – they are what England is all about.

Pythius says

Helen is such a spoil sport, there I was having a wonderful time splashing about in the Finstock village pond, which is just the right depth to keep me happy. This time I decided to play up and just stood there in the centre of the pond, daring her to come in and get me. She didn't.

The Plough Inn is great. It took Bella the lovely pub doggie and me a while to accept each other, but eventually we both settled down under Helen's table waiting for crumbs to drop at our feet. They didn't of course, due to that notice that says Do Not Feed the Dog – it seems that Joe and Martin are spoil sports too!

The two-mile walk

Finstock is criss-crossed with footpaths all crying out to be explored and enjoyed. As there is one right beside the pub, it's a great place to start. After a short (sometimes muddy) ascent, it leads to a wooden gate which opens out to a rough field and a well-worn track. This track, which is particularly well signed, leads to another gate on the right and way-sign offering a choice of directions. Take the left hand path which leads to a well-worn footpath that takes you right across a field of mustard.

Having crossed the field you will come to a point where there is a copse on your right and a small track leading through foliage straight ahead. Go straight ahead, past a private wood on the right keeping to the path that divides two fields.

When you come to the next way-marker which offers four choices, take the right-hand turn which will lead you round a well-worn path circling a wood until you come to a gate with two red posts.

Go through the gate and follow the path past a sign saying "Last turning place", and go on past houses on the right. You are now walking in Wilcote Lane and towards the centre of Ramsden. Turn right on reaching the High Street, having put the dog on its lead, and walk straight ahead, calling in at the Royal Oak pub on the right if you feel thirsty as this is a very well-run dog-friendly pub.

Walk on past the Memorial Hall and towards the edge of the village, turning right when you spot a public footpath on the right with a narrow boundary of stone walls. You are now walking on a gentle gradient towards the hill known as Mount Skippet, passing Little Garden Wood along the way.

On reaching a division of ways, bear left taking the track fenced with wire. It was at this point that Pythius suddenly darted ahead and then vanished. Within moments we heard that familiar splashing noise which told us he had found water. Yes, he had discovered the village pond. Fortunately there were no ducks in evidence so he was able to splash about to his heart's content.

On removing Pythius from the pond (not an easy task), we walked back and followed the path until we reached a field. Keeping to the right-hand edge, we discovered it finally led to the upper end of Finstock. By turning right, we could have been back at the Plough in no time, but first we needed to pay homage to T. S. Eliot by visiting Holy Trinity Church.

We got to the church by taking the second footpath sign on the left-hand side of the road after about 250 yards, which led us up the side of a field, then sharp right across a field and towards the church and its cemetery where novelist Barbara Pym is buried.

Having soaked up the atmosphere of the church, while gently reading from my complete works of T. S. Eliot, we returned to the Plough Inn by way of a wide track running beside the churchyard. As we walked, we kept the field boundary on our left. At the end, we turned left past houses and the most amazing children's wooden playground we had ever seen. It looks rather like a film set, actually. You are now approaching School Road, and just need to turn right to get you down the hill and back to the pub.

Fossebridge
The Inn at Fossebridge

The Fosse Way: a Roman road

Two-mile circular walk through idyllic countryside

The idyllic little hamlet of Fossebridge stands eight miles north of Cirencester and 11 miles south of Stow-on-the-Wold and is linked to these two towns by the A429, otherwise known as the Fosse Way, which was a Roman road. This 230-mile long road travels from Exeter to Lincoln and marked the western frontier of Roman Britain. It is thought that it may have been a defensive ditch to start with, to be filled in and used as a road later, as the word *fosse* means ditch.

The Inn at Fossebridge, as its name suggests, nestles besides a bridge over the River Coln and in a dip on the Fosse Way where it passes through the Coln Valley, just three miles out of Northleach, four miles from Bibury. Its close proximity to Chedworth means it is also just three miles from one of the most spectacular Roman villas in the country.

It's no wonder that the Romans chose to settle in this area – even during the winter months, the Coln Valley displays a breathtaking and haunting beauty, which remains gloriously unspoiled.

The inn dates back to the Georgian period and stands in four acres

of mature garden with a small lake dominating the centre. The River Coln acts as one of the garden's boundaries.

Describing the Inn at Fossebridge without resorting to superlatives is impossible. This remarkable inn is not only one of the most friendly establishments I have ever visited, it is professionally run too. It is indeed a true country retreat offering guests a chance to step back in time and enjoy old fashioned hospitality and fine food in rustic surroundings.

It goes without saying that Pythius was made really welcome and that a large bowl of water was waiting for him at the side of the bar. A jar of dog biscuits sits on the bar.

The menu is superb and creative, offering many items you wouldn't find on most menus, including several Thai dishes which are sumptuous, and the choice of real ales great.

The walk

A delightful two-mile walk that takes you and your dog through a small section of the Coln Valley begins in the inn's beautiful garden.

You begin by walking to the left-hand side of the garden with the lake on your right until you notice an exit beside a small minor road. You will also spot a wooden way-marker on the opposite side of the road pointing you towards a meadow and wooden stile.

Cross the road and climb the stile. That's almost all you need to know as you will immediately see that the many walkers who have travelled this way over the years have marked a way through the grass. All you have to do is follow in their footsteps as you pass from field to field along this lovely unspoiled valley through which a small stream meanders.

You eventually spot the roofs of houses and the last wooden stile on this part of the walk. It will appear as if the stile leads to someone's garden – worry not – it is a small green lane leading to a minor road.

This is the time to put your dog on the lead, for although it is a small road, much traffic travels this way.

On reaching the road, turn left and then left again a few yards on when you come to a way-marker guiding you back the way you have come, but on an entirely different path.

Once more, the sight of rooftops indicates the end of the path, which this time terminates at the A429, so secure the dog well before you reach this point. Now all you have to do is turn left, cross the minor road and head for the Inn at Fossebridge where a warm welcome awaits you.

Pythius says

Another glorious walk in mind-blowing countryside. Gosh what a lucky dog I am. The pub was great too. I was treated as if I was a real star – perhaps I am?

May Hill

The Yew Tree, Cliffords Mesne

Ivor Gurney, Cotswold composer and poet (1890–1917)

Three mile circular walk

We decided it was the perfect day for climbing a high hill. The sky was blue, the air crisp and our energy levels high, so we drove towards Gloucestershire and May Hill, in high spirits. Pythius knew without being told that we were all in for a real treat and he was right. Gloucestershire is indeed a magic place and May Hill is particularly idyllic and as it is 970 feet high, one of the county's highest natural vantage points. It's here that Morris men celebrate May 1st at dawn with a dance.

We chose May Hill and for several reasons, but mainly because this is one of the many Gloucestershire spots that the composer and poet Ivor Gurney walked while living in this area. The poets Robert Frost and Edward Thomas walked this hill too.

You reach May Hill by travelling the A40 in a westerly direction, past Gloucester and on for about five miles until you notice it's sign-posted on the right hand side on a minor road. A right hand turn into Yartleton Lane will take you to the official May Hill car park.

Although this hill has been walked by many famous Cotswold men, we were there to walk in the footsteps of a poet and composer whose

very soul is linked with glorious Gloucestershire spots such as this, as his moving poems convey. Gurney found great solace walking the Gloucestershire which was embedded in his soul since birth.

As his life progressed Gurney became increasingly depent on 'being in' Gloucestershire places such as May Hill, seeing them as a source of his identity and well-being. He and Gloucestershire were inextricably intertwined. Sadly his life was plagued with ill health and he was confined to a mental asylum in Kent for the last 15 years of his life. It was here that he wrote heart-breaking poems that reflected his feelings of absence and loss.

He is buried in the nearby churchyard of St Matthew's Church, Twigworth, where bunches of freshly cut flowers continue to adorn his grave. We visited his grave after the walk, clutching a splendid book of his life, *Ivor Gurney's Gloucestershire* by Eleanor M. Rawling, from which we read one of his late heart-wrenching poems, *The Songs I Had*, which grieves for the Gloucestershire that was taken away from him.

> *The Songs I had are Withered*
> *Or vanished clean*
> *there are bright tracks*
> *Where I have been.*
> *And there grow flowers*
> *For others delight*
> *Think well, O singer*
> *Still comes the night.*

It was only decent to pay homage to this prolific first world war poet who also filled the Cotswold landscape with his music which we sensed still echoes around the trees if you are prepared to suspend disbelief and listen to the melodic rustling of the leaves.

The pub

By turning right out of the car park we soon reached the dog-frendly The Yew Tree pub where we were welcomed with open arms. This pub, which is a free house, began life as a cider press several centuries ago. Its traditional bar is known for its cosy log fires that add a dancing warmth during the winter months.

The menu offers a strange mix of dishes, many of which are created from the rare breed pigs reared on the pub's own farm. Most of the vegetables come from their own garden, but as we wanted something

---

Pythius says

Having seen Helen scanning that big map which she can never fold up without getting into a real flap, I knew that we were in for a great trip.

She lays it on the floor and then uses a magnifying glass to decide where we are going to go. As she had a book about this Gloucestershire poet lying beside the map, I knew she was looking for a special place. And yes, May Hill is a special place, I loved it, particularly the wood at the end.

The pub? Oh that was fine, they were kind to me and the water they brought me was cool and crisp, almost as good as Helen's wine which she sipped with sheer pleasure.

---

light we chose dishes from the starters menu, which we washed down with a couple of glasses of an excellent merlot to celebrate the fact that this pub was classified Wine Pub of the Year in 2010.

While dogs are allowed inside in the bar area, we ate outside and enjoyed the silence that areas such as this provide. Pythius was served water within seconds of requesting it.

The walk

Although you can climb May Hill from the entrance at the car park, we decided to walk back along the road we had travelled for half a mile so that we could conquer the hill through the first entrance in Yartleton Lane. This entrance, which is a picturesque lane that begins with a series of steps, is on the right hand side and signed to May Hill. It really is the easiest walk to the summit, and though there are many other lanes and tracks you can follow, this one allows you to ascend the hill and arrive at its tree-lined peak on an easy track in less than ten minutes.

Once you have reached the top, which is a Site of Special

Scientific Interest, having passed a few wandering horses gently grazing and quite unperturbed by visitors, you can gaze out at the view, which even Pythius seemed to appreciate. Because you are now more than 900 feet above sea level, it seems as if the whole world is there for you to view – well, at least seven counties, also the Malvern Hills, the Welsh borders and even the Seven estuary which twists its way

through the landscape like a snake. This is not a time to hurry, and as seats are strategically placed around the top of the hill, you can sit and ponder, taking in its beauty at your ease.

There have always been a few trees at the very top of May Hill, however the natural pines you will see now were specially planted to commemorate the Golden Jubilee of Queen Victoria in 1887. While we were there Paul the wood cutter was gathering up the remains of one of the trees that he had felled the day before as it was diseased. Sadly there is another sick pine he has to work on shortly.

Having walked to the top of the hill, we took the pathway signed as the Wysis Way, walking down hill on a well-worn path, passing heather and gorse as we went.

On reaching the bottom, having kept a woodland on your left, you come to a gate and stile leading on downhill. Ignore this, looking instead for a stile on your right which comes into view just before you arrive at this gate. This will take you along a permitted path through a lovely unspoiled wood. Because we were visiting outside the dates when dogs must be kept on a lead because of ground-nesting birds, Pythius was allowed to run free.

The woods are delightful, with wild food plants in abundance. The path through the trees leads to the original path we walked to get to the hill. So all we had to do was to turn left when the path through the woods met the path to the hill, then right at the bottom and back to the car park.

Kelmscott
The Plough

Walking in the footsteps of William Morris

I doubt that anyone loved the Cotswolds more than William Morris, or did more to encourage members of the Arts and Crafts Movement to follow in his footsteps and help make the world a more beautiful place. Craftsman, poet, conservationist, calligrapher, printer, socialist, textile designer and dreamer of dreams, he was much influenced by the Cotswold countryside and the beautiful limestone buildings which he felt grew out of the very earth on which they stood.

From 1871 to 1896 William Morris spent his summers at Kelmscott Manor, Kelmscott, leaving an indelible mark on both this magnificent house and the surrounding countryside, which remains as unspoilt now as the year he first set his eyes on the Manor, fell in love with it, and made it his own.

To embrace all that William Morris stood for, a visit to Kelmscott Manor is highly recommended. Unfortunately dogs are not allowed inside the manor house, but they are welcomed at the local pub, The Plough, which is but a stone's throw away. They can then romp along the Thames towpath that will take you to Lechlade and St John's Bridge, if you turn right. This is the way we always go as The Swan at Radcot, which you reach by turning left at the river, only allows dogs in the garden, whereas the Trout, that stands close to the bridge at Lechlade and is 700 years old, is definitely dog-friendly, providing they remain in the section of the bar with the flagstone flooring. Besides which, the Trout is a lovely old pub, with atmosphere and great food; the Sunday roast is particularly good – generous portions too. It gets really busy during sunny weekends, so it is best to arrive early and before the crowds of walkers descend. As it has an attractive garden there is never a problem getting a table on a sunny day.

We usually visit The Plough at Kelmscott, however, which dates back to the 17th century and was William Morris's local. It's good to think of him sitting in the small bar enjoying a pint (or two) of ale before ambling down the Thames path, or simply returning to the Manor House.

The Plough had to undergo massive reno-vations when the 2007 floods filled it with river water. Indeed it was closed for a couple of years while the damage was made good. It is lovely to see it open again.

Visit it during the winter and you can roast yourself by a roaring log fire while enjoying your food and sipping a jolly good local ale from the selection always on tap.

A bowl of water is placed outside the main door for visiting canines, though they are welcome to sit in the bar with their masters if they wish. The food is fine; there is a well-balanced menu that offers every-thing from sandwiches to hot cooked main meals at a reasonable price.

The walk

If we feel lazy we turn right on reaching the Thames, having walked the little lane to the left of the pub that leads to the Thames Path, and just amble beside the river until we feel it is time to turn round. When we want a longer walk we make our way to Lechlade and then on to the remarkable little medieval St John the Baptist Church at Inglesham, which owes its unspoiled look to William Morris. Sometimes we take the car and drive to the centre of Lechlade and walk to the church from there: it is just over a mile away.

St John the Baptist Church, Inglesham, is located just above the water meadows outside Lechlade, adjacent to the confluence of the River Thames, River Coln and the Severn Canal. According to Richard Taylor, BBC Four's presenter of *Churches: How to Read Them*, it is his favourite out of the hundreds of churches he has visited. He describes it as a totally unassuming building set in the middle of the countryside.

But don't be put off by its humble exterior; this church boasts Anglo Saxon carvings and medieval wall paintings spanning 600 years, among them an Anglo Saxon carving of Mother and Child. Much of

Pythius says

Ever since I first walked the Kelmscott area I have wondered if that clever Mr Morris had a dog of his own, and if so, whether I was walking in their footprints. It would be nice to think he had, but Helen shakes her head when I ask, saying he was far too busy to look after a canine companion. I think she is wrong – but I doubt I will ever be able to prove it.

this church dates back to the 13th century, but includes remains of an earlier church. It is also furnished with wooden box pews which fascinated William Morris.

When Morris discovered a major restoration was planned for this church in the 1880s he campaigned successfully to save the building, which stood only a few miles from his Kelmscott home.

The church was declared redundant in 1979 and is now in the safe hands of the Care of Churches Conservation Trust. Be assured, it is

well worth visiting and there are no notices saying NO DOGS so placing Pythius on his lead we allowed him to enter with us. He was as overwhelmed by its history as we were.

From Lechlade you get to the church by walking over Ha'penny Bridge and taking the right hand turning towards the Thames, keeping the river on your right-hand side as you walk forward; it's just a matter of following it past Inglesham Round House, then over a small wooden bridge. You can't miss the Round House which sits on a bend in the river on the far bank, because as its name suggests, it really is a round house.

The track which will then guide you to the small road and the church is clearly marked by the hundreds of footsteps that have passed this way before. You can't miss it. On reaching a gate, turn right, the church is now just a few yards away. Be assured, it really is a treasure not to be missed.

King's Stanley
The King's Head

Artist Sir Stanley Spencer and the village of Leonard Stanley

Three-mile circular walk

Stanley Spencer, one of the greatest British artists of the first part of the 20th century, is mainly associated with Cookham, which he considered his spiritual haven and where he spent most of his life. There is another place associated with his name, however – the charming little Cotswold village of Leonard Stanley which can be found nestling below the wooded Cotswold escarpment, two miles west of Stroud.

A blue plaque, funded in part by the Stonehouse History Group, was erected on the wall of the White Hart pub in October 2011 to commemorate the two years Spencer stayed there (September 1939 – May 1941) when seeking refuge from his traumatic second marriage to Patricia Preece in 1937. His stay in the Cotswolds with his friends Daphne and George Charlton began as a painting holiday, but he extended his visit to two years, when his friendship with Daphne developed into a passionate love affair. Spencer created several prominent paintings whilst staying in a small room at the White Hart, which included Us in Gloucestershire and The Wool Shop.

Sadly the White Hart doesn't open during the day time now, so you can either visit during the evening or just stop and stare at the blue plaque on the wall and the attractive little Norman church opposite that Spencer would have looked out on from his window. As the White Hart was closed during our visit to the area, we stopped for refreshments at the King's Head in the adjoining village of King's Stanley. It's just a stone's throw from a small public car park.

The King's Head, King's Stanley

Both King's Stanley and Leonard Stanley are close to the Cotswold Way and can be reached by taking a turn off the A419. You can't miss this pub where we stopped for lunch as it is a large imposing cream coloured building in the centre of the village.

We were delighted to find that despite its size, it had a comfortably homely feel reminiscent of pubs renovated in the 1970s, though the restaurant has been refurbished recently. The staff were particularly friendly, so were the assembled customers who appeared fascinated by the way Pythius looked around the main bar area with an air of one who knows what he is looking for, and then took himself to a table in the far corner where he settled down to sleep. We had no alternative but to follow him.

Had we wanted to, we could have visited the pub's coffee shop, which opens for travellers at 8.30 am and serves wonderful home-made cakes. But Uncle John and I needed a warming bowl of soup which was served promptly, tasted delicious and was reasonably priced. We washed this down with a couple of glasses of Black Rat premium cider, for no particular reason except I had never tried it before and it was ages since I had enjoyed a glass of traditional English scrumpy. It didn't disappoint.

The walk

Leave your car in King Stanley's little car park opposite the King's Head, turn right into High Street and keep walking straight past the houses – you will eventually reach Castle Street and then Woodland View and be making your way towards a tree-lined lane. Ignore foot-path signs on the right-hand side and keep going as the lane begins to curve towards the right past a few farm houses. A little way further you

Pythius says

Gosh, you should have seen Helen's face when she realised just how steep that narrow path down through the wooded escarpment was. I was really worried that she wouldn't make it. Uncle John was fine and marched on like a trooper, whereas Helen kept stumbling, finding it rather difficult. All I can say is, thank goodness the ground was dry. I am sure it would have been very slippery if it was muddy. Me? Oh I'm always fine when faced with a steep slope; after all, I have four big paws which keep me well balanced.

I liked the pub and the people in it, but was too exhausted to do much more than tuck myself under the table and sleep while Uncle John and Helen enjoyed their well-earned lunch.

will discover a metal post beside the lane filled with signs, including one to the right signed to The Blackbirds, which is the direction you take. At this point there is no permitted access to motor vehicles so the dog can be safely let off the lead.

The views that appear from time to time through gaps in the hedge as you ascend the escarpment are spectacular. You can now look down on the village you left. It's at this point that will you realise how far you have climbed even though you don't appear to have been on an arduous journey.

You eventually take a turn to the right when you come to a Permitted Byway sign. It takes you through a wooded area and then down, down, down a narrow path that seems to go on forever. It finally levels out and passes through open countryside and fields of sheep. This is Gypsy Lane and leads straight to Leonard Stanley. Turn left at the end of the lane and the White Hart where Spencer stayed comes into view. Having viewed the blue plaque, turn round and walk to the right down Church Road turning right when it meets Marsh Lane, then walk just a few yards until you spot Dozule Close on the left and the roofs of houses in King's Stanley which is now under half a mile away.

Look out for a metal gate and way sign which will direct you across a field and to a small footbridge that spans a brook. Cross the bridge and you will eventually come out at Woodland View. Turn right and you are back on the lane you first walked and close to the King's Head.

It's worth noting that King's Stanley and Leonard Stanley have been awarded the status of communities where 'Walkers are Welcome', which is a nationally recognised scheme that aims to boost the local economy by attracting walkers to the area. Many of the kissing gates and footbridges on the walks circulating these villages are maintained by Cotswold Voluntary Wardens, who patrol the footpaths regularly and help keep them in good order. The wardens also include the Stanleys in their guided walks.

Malmesbury

The Smoking Dog

Two-mile circular river walk

On learning about a monk who fitted wings to his arms and legs and attempted to fly from the top of a Cotswold abbey, only to crash to the ground breaking both legs, I wanted to know more, which is why we decided to visit the beautiful hilltop town of Malmesbury, which sits at the southern edge of the Cotswold Hills.

This is the place where Eilmer, an 11th-century monk, made his attempt to fly, but after keeping airborne for just 200 yards, plunged to the ground. It seems he was inspired to attempt this feat having read the Greek fable of Daedalus, the ingenious inventor who made wings from wax and feathers for his son Icarus. On flying too close to the sun however, Icarus's wings melted, plunging him into the sea. But this didn't put Eilmer off. He'd watched the birds swooping and gliding around the abbey and assumed that with wings it was possible, so he

constructed wings for himself, fixed them to his arms and feet, then leapt from the abbey tower. His wings didn't melt, but like Icarus, he fell from the sky, crushing both legs as he hit the ground. It's said that he blamed his fall on the lack of a tail.

Although Eilmer remained a cripple for the rest of his life, he did plan a second attempt and would have probably flown again had the abbot not banned him from such foolish acts. A 20th-century stained glass window in the abbey shows the monk with both wings in his hands.

We decided to see this window and also check out Malmesbury's magnificent abbey where Eilmer attempted to fly. Founded as a Benedictine monastery about 676, it dominates the skyline and has a long and colourful history, also a spacious garden that's reputed to contain the largest rose garden in England.

On entering the abbey with Pythius, we were welcomed warmly by the many volunteers meeting and greeting visitors. No one turned Pythius away, leaving us all free to explore this remarkable place with Pythius padding cautiously at our side.

The Smoking Dog

Having discovered a 17th-century pub in the High Street called The Smoking Dog, we didn't bother to look further; besides, it had a large sign outside welcoming both dogs and children. We never did manage to discover how it got its name, but we did find a fine assortment of real ales on tap, including Abbot Ale. Although a small pub, it's nicely fitted out and the staff are both professional and friendly. Pythius was welcome inside, but as the sun was shining and the Smoking Dog is the only pub in town with a family beer garden, we ate there under the shade of a tree.

The food is impressive, for although we only ordered filled baguettes, they were nicely prepared and the filling was generous. And yes, water was provided for Pythius.

The walk

The walk begins in Conygre Mead, reached from the main car park. Keeping the River Avon to your right, walk through a kissing gate and

Pythius says

There were times when we walked besides the river Helen put me on my lead as she didn't want me to disturb the nesting birds in the reeds. I didn't like that much; all that cool inviting water rippling along, just waiting to be disturbed by a Border collie. But that is how it is and we did find lots of places where she allowed me to play without restrictions.

Loved the pub and the little garden at the back, though we did have to climb down some rather steep steps to get there. As water was provided in plenty for their canine visitors I was happy to navigate them, drink my water, then put my paws under the table until Helen and Uncle John had finished their meal.

towards the abbey. It is an idyllic spot to walk as the river gently ripples through the overhanging branches dipping their leaves in the water.

On reaching the road, cross bearing slightly right over the bridge and descend a set of steps that lead to a stile. Walk on until you come to a division of paths, take the right-hand track and head towards the right side of the field where you will discover a little gate and a small wooden bridge. Note that you might well encounter a few cows at this point, but they are somnolent beasts that appear accustomed to visitors as they ignored us completely. Take the left-hand path that follows the river bank to a stile and small footbridge and walk the lane past Wynyard Mill, turning right after reaching the bowls club. Now, keeping your dog on a lead, follow St John's Street to Lower High Street.

You will now spot the Memorial Gardens; go through the main gates and bear left along the path parallel to St John's Bridge, re-joining the road opposite Avon Mills, an impressive red-brick Victorian building.

By turning right you will now come to a permissive path that takes you back to the river bank. Keeping to the path, cross the next stile and various footbridges, until the path leaves the river bank. Now keep a hedge on your right-hand side until you come to a gap in the corner of the field and a small stone bridge.

The path is now paved and takes you to a footbridge, turning left at a T-junction look out for Betty Geezer's Steps on your right. These superb stone steps will lead you to Abbey Row, with the Civic Trust garden on your left. By crossing the road now you will end up at the abbey, which really is worth exploring before walking through the Cloister Garden. By turning left down more steps and then right along Mill Lane you will end up at the car park where your walk began.

Minster Lovell

The Old Swan

This one-mile walk to the ruins of Minster Lovell Hall and back can be extended to take in the village of Crawley

The idyllic little village of Minster Lovell stands on the edge of the Oxfordshire Cotswolds, three miles west of Witney.

The moment you walk through the main door of the Old Swan Inn, you will know you are entering a special place. It is one of those remarkable old hotels that has been stylishly refurbished in places, yet manages to retain an atmospheric 'olde worlde' feel. A roaring log fire greets you in the winter months and during the summer months the main door to the bar is kept open to allow the outside in.

The large garden at the rear, with its well-tended vegetable patch, offers you a chance to dine al fresco if you wish.

It goes without saying that a warm welcome to both you and your canine friend is assured the moment you enter. Indeed dogs are so welcome, they have their own pit-stop designed especially for them by

the bar that displays a super fresco-style wall painting of a smiling dog at floor level so that the dogs can see it. Beside the picture is a bowl of chilled water and an assortment of doggie biscuits for your dog to discover. And if your dog doesn't wander into the bar and find these treats for itself, staff will arrive at your table clutching a handful of doggie treats. In other words, dogs visiting this splendid hostelry are thoroughly spoiled. There are dog-friendly rooms too for those who wish to stay overnight with their canine friends.

If we arrive early enough during the winter months, Pythius tries to tuck himself into a corner near the fire and watch the flames dance. He is allowed anywhere in the extensive bar area at the front where we can settle in comfortable chairs, admire the beamed ceiling and the flag-stone floors and look forward to being thoroughly spoiled.

The food is superb, freshly cooked and beautifully served. Each plate looks as if it has leapt out of a glossy foodie magazine. Naturally such treats don't come cheaply, but once again this is an example of getting what you pay for. Auntie Liz and I consider it the place where we can spoil ourselves when we feel in need of a real treat. We usually choose roast beef with traditional trimmings, which comes with crunchy roast potatoes and an impressive selection of fresh seasonal vegetables – many which have been harvested from the garden at the back. The beef is served medium, with just enough pink to get the gastric juices going. The food is so good we often eat in silence as we savour every mouthful. As Brakspear real ales are on tap, it is doubly good. It is worth noting that this lovely 15th-century inn is now transforming itself into a child-friendly pub – a play area in the main garden which comes complete with a fascinating guinea pig enclosure is now available to keep young visitors amused.

The walk

On leaving the Old Swan Inn, having been given permission to leave our car in the car park, we cross the road and with our backs to the inn, walk left for just a few steps towards a gate the other side of the road that provides access to the village cricket field. Keep walking left towards the next field, keeping the boundary on your left. This adjoining field is particularly muddy during winter months, due in part to the cattle that graze the area you will be walking.

You soon reach a little wooden bridge and kissing gates which will take you to a path that leads to St Kenelm's Church and the mysterious ruins of Minster Lovell Hall which stands beside the River Windrush. Two large fish ponds which once supplied the household with fresh fish can be found on the west and south-east of the ruins. Although there has been a manor house here since the 12th century, the major part of the ruins you will see today date back to the 15th century. They were built by William Baron of Lovell and Holland who, at the time, was considered the richest man in England. Much of the building was dismantled in 1747, many parts being demolished for building stone. The weather-worn ruins that remain in this unspoiled landscape have a haunting beauty and harbour a strange sense of melancholy. When viewed from a distance on an autumnal day with mist drifting through its crumbling ruins it is a moving sight.

And yes, the ruins are said to be haunted by the first Viscount Lovell who is thought to have died of starvation in an underground room where he was hiding, having been declared guilty of treason after the battle of Bosworth. He and his little dog were thought to have died together, trapped in a basement room, as a man's skeleton sprawled across table, with the bones of a little dog at his feet, were discovered. His ghost is said to have been seen rising from the river on a horse.

Another ghost, a young woman dressed in a white wedding gown and with flowers in her hair, has been seen slowly descending an invisible stair-case. She is thought to have been playing hide-and-seek with her

Pythius says

It's no good me pretending to be brave when we go to places like those ruins that Helen insists on visiting now and again. As soon as we enter the grounds I get a tingly feeling all the way down my back which I really don't like. It frightens me. I can feel my fur standing on end and my teeth begin

to jangle. And when she declares she wants me to pose among the ruins for a photo, that really is the last straw. Helen does push her luck sometimes – but I did pose of course, how could I do otherwise? She is such a bossy boots.

The pub however is great, the staff make such a fuss of me, and where else would you find a doggie pit-stop complete with a dish of my favourite biscuits which I seldom get to enjoy midday? A great pub indeed.

husband, and hid in an old chest where she was trapped, dying in this living tomb when she was not found. Take your time exploring the ruins; there is much to see and members of the public are free to wander where they will. So are their canine friends.

It's worth taking a look at the church next to the ruins while in the area and walking back via the little lane at the front of the church. This will mean you have to keep your dog on a lead, but it will take you past some charming thatched cottages as you make your way back to the Old Swan.

For a longer walk you can follow the river, crossing a small foot-bridge a little further on which puts the river on your left-hand side. Follow the way-signs and you will arrive at the village of Crawley where The Lamb Inn is a great dog-friendly pub.

Moreton-in-Marsh

The Bell Inn

J. R. R. Tolkien

Three-mile circular walk

After painstaking research, members of the Tolkien Society concluded that The Bell Inn, High Street, Moreton-in-Marsh was Tolkien's inspiration for The Prancing Pony pub, Middle Earth's most famous hostelry in his classic *The Lord of the Rings*, and that Moreton-in-Marsh provided the basis for the town of Bree that stood at an old meeting of the ways.

Anyone who has visited this old coaching inn will no doubt agree that the Bell Inn may well have acted as the model for the Prancing Pony as it is a three-storey building with a meeting room and an entrance via a courtyard which the hobbits entered one cold, rainy night.

Yes, there have been alterations to the Bell Inn over the years, but it has an atmosphere that links perfectly to the Prancing Pony. It also appears to be a place that would appeal to an Oxford don such as Tolkien, who would no doubt have enjoyed sitting at one of the window tables looking out on the Fosse Way, the ancient Roman road that runs through the town. Tolkien is said to have visited the inn when travelling from Oxford to Evesham to visit his brother and would have therefore known it well.

He would have also been familiar with the 16th-century Four Shire Stone, situated just two miles east of Moreton-in-Marsh, which marks the point where four shires used to meet. Now, after local government reorganisation in the 1970s, there are only three shires that meet here. The boundary of Worcestershire is now further east, leaving Oxfordshire, Gloucestershire and Warwickshire to meet at this point. It is thought that this nine-foot-high stone created from Cotswold stone was Tolkien's inspiration for the Three Farthing Stone, a central point where three farthings met in Lord of the Rings.

Although Pythius knew nothing of the Bell Inn's history, has no knowledge of Middle Earth and has never met a hobbit, he walked

inside with confidence and enjoyed his stay immensely, particularly when a lovely woman artist walked over to speak to him and having patted his head called him a very handsome dog. This moment became even more precious, when we met her again in the street. She was rushing towards us waving one of our Paws books in her hand which she had just purchased from the local bookshop. She wanted Pythius to sign it. A nice moment, particularly as we had just left an inn that one of England's most famous writers had immortalised.

Pythius says

May I begin by advising anyone wishing to take this walk to wear Wellington boots if walking during a rainy period. I don't have boots so at the point where we were leaving the path through Lower Rye Farm and into a field I had to place my paws in several inches of real farmyard muck. The smell was something that even a Border collie finds objectionable.

The pub was terrific, the staff were really friendly and even offered me a biscuit to eat while Helen and Auntie Caroline ate their lunch. And the lovely lady who talked to me, then rushed out and bought one of my books – well what can I say? She was a real sweetie.

The food we were served at the Bell Inn by the way was simply scrumptious, and the choice of real ales imaginative. I'd go as far as to say it rates as one of the best pub meals I have had for some considerable time.

The walk

Leave the pub, turn right and cross the A429 that passes through the centre of the town. After the junction with the A44, turn left into Church Street. Walk past the church and go on a little further to a lane called Old Town and follow it round past a long metal fence. At the end of the fence turn right to walk alongside some very well kept allotments. You will now come to a small lane. Turn left into the lane, then right over a small footbridge that straddles a little brook.

Having crossed the bridge, walk across a well-worn track that goes straight through an open field and onto a path that passes a sheep pasture on the left which is secured by an electric fence and make your way to the first stile, having passed Dunstall Farm. Unfortunately this stile is not dog-friendly. We finally managed to lift Pythius over, but it was with difficulty and we certainly could not have managed if he had been a larger and less nimble dog.

You will meet another stile, but this one is dog-friendly and leads to Frogmore Farm. Pass the farm buildings and take a bridle path to the right that continues to pass farm buildings. It will take you to the A429, which is quite a busy road, so take care to place the dog firmly on the lead. Cross the road and take the bridleway opposite which will lead you past Maidenhill Farm, then on to Lower Rye Farm, which is well stocked with cattle and sheep. Plastic lambing sheds had been erected when we passed this farm, where little day-old lambs were cuddling

down in the straw. We also
passed several cattle sheds.
Although the right of way appears
to go straight through the farm,
we took what seemed like a better
option of a concrete path which
winds round to the left and eventually bears to the right, where
even more cattle and cattle sheds
can be seen, so you need to keep
your dog under tight control.

There comes a point when the
concrete path comes to an end
and you are facing a field where
the cattle graze. This proved a
rather difficult moment as there
was electric fencing to pass under
before turning right into the field, and the earth at this point was thick
with mud mixed with rather a lot of more slurry than we would have
cared to walk through. But we did of course; so did Pythius, though I
don't think he liked the experience any more than we did.

Follow the path with the farm behind you and a hedge on your left.
The marked path then goes left over a tricky stile which caused Pythius
more difficulties.

Now we were heading for the Monarch's Way, recognisable by the
little circular sticker on the way signs, decorated with the picture of a
royal boat. Having crossed a little stream you will meet this way in the
middle of the next field. Turn right at this point and follow the well-
worn path marked generously with way signs, which will take you back
to Moreton and past the new community hospital on the far right.
Some of the way markers are no longer vertical, but when in doubt go
straight ahead. Moreton-in-Marsh's church spire will be in view now
and providing you follow the signs, the next track will take you down
a green lane and a small road on the right which will take you to the
A44 and the High Street.

Nether Westcote

The Feathered Nest Inn

Ancient ridge and furrow fields

Two-mile circular walk that takes you through two ancient ridge and furrow fields

The Feathered Nest Inn, Nether Westcote, is a fine example of how a pub can be completely refurbished, yet look as if it has remained undisturbed for years. You will find it tucked away round a corner of one of three villages bearing the Nether name that are found on the eastern side of the A424 between Burford and Stow-on-the-Wold.

Seen from the outside, it looks rather like the house that Jack built, but when you walk through the door into the first of many small intimate areas, all beautifully furnished, it is obvious that this is one of the most stylish pubs for miles around. Even on a cold grey day when the sun hides behind the clouds, it is stunning and so is the view from the patio. This inn, which began life as a malt house, looks down on the Evenlode valley. With its lush undulating landscape with scattered wooded areas and dwellings built from the honey-coloured Cotswold stone that marks this area as both enchanting and unforgettable, the valley is quite magical. Some describe the view as one of the most beautiful in the country. It is certainly quite breathtaking.

Dogs are welcome at The Feathered Nest providing they are happy to place their paws under the tables in the second level bar or outside in the garden. A superb water bowl that is so posh it ought to have a designer label is offered immediately the dog enters. What Pythius didn't expect was a doggie bag too, but I will let him tell you about that.

When Auntie Liz ordered a Cotswold pasty for her lunch she was warned that all food is freshly cooked and it would take at least 20 minutes – which as far as she was concerned was fine. The atmosphere was so relaxing, the wood burning fire so warm and snug, and the staff so friendly, we would have been happy to have waited even longer as we sipped our glasses of Hook Norton's Best Bitter.

When our food did arrive (the Cotswold pasty and my fish and chips), it came served on rustic wooden platters and tasted absolutely

delicious. It certainly confirmed that the many food awards this pub has won since it opened a couple of years ago are well deserved. One word of advice: As this inn has now become so popular, do phone to book a table if you aim to visit during the weekend.

The walk

This two-mile circular walk will allow you to take a bridle-path on the left virtually next to the Feathered Nest that leads you into the heart of the view you enjoyed from the garden of the pub. One of the delightful things about this walk is the fact that although it is downhill all the way to the bottom, the ascent on the way back is painless. Not once on the return leg did Auntie Liz or I stop and pretend we were admiring the view, when in truth on other walks this has been an excuse to pause and get our breath back! As for Pythius, well he just runs backwards and forwards with no effort at all, regardless of the terrain we are climbing.

Much of this walk takes you down picturesque tree-lined green lanes, and towards the end you pass medieval ridge and furrow fields – the name given to the regular humps and troughs that can sometimes be found on ancient fields, an effect that was achieved by the ploughing of ancient family-owned plots over a long period of time. Another clue to the many centuries this land has been farmed is the remarkable mix of bushes and trees intertwined in the hedgerows.

The walk starts by turning left outside the pub and walking a few yards to a bridleway sign. As there was evidence that horses had passed this way, do keep a watchful eye on your dog as you walk this track.

Throughout the walk you will pass through countless sturdy kissing gates made by Cotswold volunteers; do admire their handiwork as you pass through as these gates are so well made they will last for years.

This walk is so well signed that it is a matter of walking this peaceful track for about two miles. When you come to a little wooden bridge spanning a small stream on the left after walking about a quarter of a mile, turn right into a green lane that runs alongside a large field and parallel to the track you have just left. When it meets up with the track again a way-marker points you to the left, and along another track. Walk on for a short distance and then turn left when you arrive at a broken wooden stile. Initially you may wonder if this is the right way as the path is narrow and slightly overgrown, but be assured it is. Just walk on and you will soon come to the first of two large fields with the humps and troughs from medieval days.

This is the really exciting part of this walk, for you are walking across medieval ridges and furrow fields that give a rippled effect to the landscape. The fields have only retained the undulations created by the medieval farmer's plough because they were left to become grassland that has never been ploughed. Each of these ridges would have probably been a family plot. This amazing topography is the result of ploughing with a non-reversible plough round and round a strip of land over and over again. Such fields are rare and certainly worth visiting.

When you reach the second field, a way-sign on the kissing gate will send you straight ahead, when in fact you need to walk diagonally over

---

Pythius says

I still can't believe it. When we were settling at our table and I was adjusting my paws so that they would be comfortable, the lovely Amanda Timmer, who runs the inn with her husband Tony, came up to me, patted my head, talked to me for a few moments then handed me a carrier bag filled with "Doggie Goodies". Apparently they are all part of the Green Fields range of elegant and wholesome dog products, the same firm that created that "posh water bowl" which was placed before me.

One bottle was a spray to make my coat shine and make me smell sweet if I roll in things I shouldn't roll in (like fox droppings) and another was a yummy bag of gourmet doggie biscuits. Whilst I have sometimes been presented with a bag containing leftovers from Helen's lunch, I have NEVER, EVER been presented with my VERY OWN DOGGIE BAG. What a lucky dog I am. Apparently it was given to me when they discovered who I am as a way of congratulating me on my contribution to the Paws books. How about that then!

the field, as we soon discovered after finding no passable exit in the corner of the field we were directed to. The kissing gate you need is at the end of the hedge towards the middle of the field where there is yet another kissing gate next to a fence created from wooden posts that continue to divide the fields.

This is the point where you must put the dog on a lead as you will be walking over fields occupied by sheep. Little black diamonds appear on the way-signs now, indicating this path is part of the Diamond Way. Once you pass a farmhouse on the right and have gone through a couple of metal gates you will be approaching the road, and your dog should be kept on a lead.

On reaching the road, you will see the Church of St Mary the Virgin, which was almost entirely rebuilt from 1876, that sits in the centre of Church Westcote. Having explored this lovely little church which is rather like Dr Who's Tardis in that it appears bigger on the inside than the outside, turn towards Nether Westcote and walk towards the Feathered Nest. On your way you will pass the Tattle (the name of the green between the church and Nether Westcote) where you will see a circular Panoramic Stone erected in 2002 to celebrate the Queen's 50th anniversary. It marks the direction and distance in miles to all local villages that can be seen within this panoramic view of the Evenlode Valley.

Nympsfield

The Rose and Crown Inn

A little bit of Archers' fantasy

followed by a one-and-a-half mile walk

If I admitted that Pythius and I took Uncle John to Ambridge where we enjoyed a meal and a pint of real ale in the Bull, readers familiar with the antics of the Archer family will assume I am losing my marbles. Ambridge is a fictional village that belongs to BBC Radio 4 and Borsetshire. It is not a charming rural Cotswold village situated in the heart of Gloucestershire, a few miles from Stroud. Or is it?

Think Brigadoon and you will be close to understanding this conundrum. Brigadoon is the magical Scottish village in the musical of that name, which comes to life just once in every hundred years. The Cotswold village of Nympsfield is the village that transformed itself

into Ambridge for just one day – the 6th of July 1985, to be exact. The transformation was the residents' way of commemorating the 800-year anniversary of their first vicar to the parish. To add an air of authenticity to the day, members of the Archers' cast were invited to join in the celebrations by entering the village on a horse-drawn brewery dray.

When dusk settled that day, residents removed the sign of The Bull from the Rose and Crown Inn, took the Ambridge village store sign down from their village store and post office and allowed the local convent to shed its Grey Gable look. One day of fantasy and Nympsfield returned to normal and was firmly fixed back in Gloucestershire rather than Borsetshire.

Nympsfield is a charming rural Gloucestershire village located six miles south-west of Stroud on the path of a Roman Road. The Rose and Crown, which dominates the main street, is a 400-year-old pub built of Cotswold limestone. Addicts of The Archers, however, will be delighted to know that it really does resemble The Bull in all respects. It has a comfortable unspoilt feel, the atmosphere is friendly, and the beams are festooned with dried hops. At the rear there's a charming little restaurant which really could have come straight from The Bull. Sitting in the main bar area it was easy to imagine Freda cooking in the little kitchen and Jolene behind the bar serving pints of Shires to the Grundy family. It's no wonder that the residents decided to transform it for a day. It is a perfect match for The Bull. There is even a framed sign saying PARK YOUR FERGUSON HERE hanging close to the main bar.

Pythius says:

Bless her, Helen gets so excited when she discovers an unusual reason for visiting somewhere in the Cotswolds. When she learned that Nympsfield once transformed itself into the fictional village of Ambridge there was no stopping her – we just had to go and visit.

Well, she had her dream, we did sit in a pub that resembled The Bull, and we did pass tractors driving down the main street, just as she assumed they would in Ambridge. How excited she was on discovering this enchanting little place.

I was thrilled to discover that a dog's dinner menu was available. Never has that happened before – it made me feel so important and the pig's ear was both crunchy and tasty.

The walk? Oh yes, that was fine, just wish that they had taken a longer route so that we could have passed one of the lakes and I could have dipped my paws in the water.

There are differences though, the main one being the blackboard menu for Dog's Dinners – YES – Dog's Dinners! That is something that The Bull certainly doesn't have. In fact, this is the first time we have ever visited a pub where Pythius has been offered the chance of selecting lunch from a menu written especially for him. He chose a crispy pig's ear and munched away quite happily while we chose food from the specials menu. Although this is a rural pub, the  food equals anything you will find in a gastro pub. Uncle John chose grilled sardines which arrived glistening with oil and served with garlic aioli. I enjoyed lamb's liver, served with a mountain of fresh seasonal vegetables and creamy mashed potatoes. The prices were reasonable and the food beautifully served.

Although there were four real ales to choose from, it was no contest as the Wickwar Brewing Company's Cotswold Way was on tap. Being but a couple of miles from the Cotswold Way, and having often enjoyed this tipple's refreshing qualities, this was the one for us. Pythius drank from a water bowl strategically placed on the floor for all visiting canines.

Lunch proved a delightful experience for us all during our dream visit to The Archers' territory.

The walk

On leaving the pub we made for Woodchester Park which is owned by the National Trust and just a mile away from Nympsfield off the B4066 Stroud to Dursley road. It is a glorious secluded valley with a mansion and a chain of five man-made lakes fringed by woodland and pasture.

Park your car in the official National Trust car park, and you will discover there are three different walks to choose from which are clearly colour-marked throughout the park.

The Woodland Walk that leads to a high point and comes close to the Mansion is just 1.7 miles long. This is marked with blue arrows.

The Boathouse Walk is 3.5 miles long and, as its name suggests, takes you past the boathouse and one of the lakes. This is marked with orange arrows.

The Valley Walk, marked with red arrows, is 7 miles long, offering the chance to explore the entire park, its lakes and woodland.

Having eaten so well at the Rose and Crown, we went for the first walk, and ambled along well marked paths, that gently lead us to a high vantage point. As it came so close to the mansion, we took a short detour to view it.

The mansion is a Grade 1 listed building built in French Gothic revival style in Cotswold limestone. It is untouched by time or the modern world. The carvings in the mansion are among the finest of their kind in the world as the magnificent gargoyles decorating its exterior suggest.

Apparently the work on this building took so long that after 16 years' work, the builders left in 1870, leaving their tools behind and many of the rooms unfinished. Inside there are doors that lead nowhere and corridors that end abruptly. The trust that owns the building is now using trainee craftsmen to undertake repairs and preservation. Its doors are opened to visitors, but not on a daily basis. Opening times can be found on the park's website at www.woodchestermansion.org.uk

Ozleworth

The Royal Oak, Wotton under Edge

Wild garlic

Have you ever walked through a valley filled with wild garlic? Stopped and stared at a dense carpet of little white flowers dancing among the trees, and having taken in the view, wondered just why this remarkable little plant has proliferated so?

Such was our experience when we visited the valley of Ozleworth during the middle of May when wild garlic was in full bloom. Gosh what a sight – it was mesmerising – like one of those strangely remote valleys that so impressed J. B. Priestley during his journey through the Cotswolds. In fact, the white blooms were so prolific it would have been easy to mistake their flowers for a light smattering of snow.

The pub

On our next walk to this idyllic valley we aim to take a picnic, but on this occasion we drove three miles west through narrow country roads to Wotton-under-Edge where we discovered the Royal Oak Inn, a large whitewashed building with its own garden and car park that is situated in Haw Street. Pythius was welcome to join us for lunch in the bar area, but the sun was shining so brightly that the garden at the back of the pub next to the car park seemed a better option.

Although the menu proved quite basic, our meals were well cooked and presented attractively. It goes without saying Pythius was presented with a large bowl of chilled water, which he lapped up with enthusiasm. We ate in silence as the memory of that beautiful valley was still dancing in our heads as we recalled the beauty that surrounded us when we walked the valley floor, thick with wild garlic, primroses, cowslips, bluebells and dandelions. I mention dandelions because they

added a striking splash of deep yellow to the landscape that contrasted wonderfully with the delicate white garlic flowers.

I guess Ozleworth would be classified as a hamlet if it didn't have a small church. The village stands 18 miles south of Gloucester and 20 miles south-west of Cirencester. Apparently there was a time when a large community lived in Ozleworth valley working on the mills powered by the little Avon River. Now all that's left to suggest this land was once heavily populated is just a little row of cottages, a manor house and a small Norman church. Actually that suited us well. We chose this walk because we wanted to get away from the Easter traffic, holiday-makers and all that Bank Holidays represent. We couldn't have chosen a more perfect place. It was so peaceful; only songbirds and the buzzing of bees broke the silence, which seemed apt as the name Ozleworth was

---

Pythius says

What fun we had. Gosh what a lucky dog I am, even Helen joined me in the stream now and again while Uncle John watched little black tadpoles with waggy tails swimming round and round in circles in the shadows under a little wooden bridge. I think this was the most beautiful walk I have ever shared with Uncle John and Helen. Helen has promised to take me back to the valley in the autumn when the colours are changing. Her plan is to take a picnic in her back pack next time which we will eat besides the stream.

originally the name for an enclosure frequented by blackbirds and there were certainly plenty of them – woodpeckers too.

The walk

The walk took us down rutted tracks, bridleways, the edge of an established woodland and alongside a small stream that delighted Pythius who leapt in and out of the cool water while we took in the views.

As to directions, let me just say that you begin and end your walk at map reference ST 792934 which takes you to a space to park the car besides a road which seems to be in the middle of nowhere.

A sign for Church Bridle Path takes you through a wooden gate on the left. Take that path keeping a rather smart metal fence on your right until you come to a kissing gate that lets you into a field and down past the remaining cottages of Ozleworth. Several sheep and their lambs were there when we walked this way so Pythius was firmly fixed to his lead until we reached the cottages and on to a bridle path on the left. This guided us towards a glorious circular walk that should not be hurried. It is so clearly marked with yellow arrows we didn't get lost, ending up after a couple of miles at the original kissing gate where we started our descent into the valley and the field of sheep.

Wild garlic (allium ursinium)

Wild garlic provides similar health benefits to cultivated garlic and all parts of the plant can be eaten, most particularly the leaves which add a magic ingredient to salads and stir-fries. Its bulb is not divided into cloves but that's OK as it is quite small and a little more difficult to harvest. Far better to enjoy the leaves and the flowers, then leave the plant to die back and rest until the following spring. Once it is established in your garden you will find it propagates itself very easily. In fact it can be quite invasive if growing in conditions similar to those in Ozleworth Valley.

Prestbury
The Plough Inn

The most haunted village in Gloucestershire

Three mile circular walk

You will find the charming village of Prestbury, with its thatched and timbered cottages, on the north-east fringe of Cheltenham. It was made part of the Cheltenham Borough in 1991 following a boundary change.

Apparently more paranormal activities have been experienced here than almost any other village in England. Only Pluckley in Kent is said to boast more ghosts haunting its streets. It is, therefore, an excellent place to visit during the build-up to Hallowe'en if you want to match a walk with the seasons.

Having parked your car in the small public car park just off Mill Street, an ideal pub to visit before or after your walk is the 17th-century Plough Inn in Mill Street. Said to have begun life as a bakery, it stands opposite the 12th-century St Mary's Church where the ghostly Black

Abbot is said to reside.

This delightful thatched pub serves scrumptious basic pub grub at a very reasonable price, and a fine selection of real ales, which are all served with a smile. It also boasts a picturesque garden at the rear.

During our visit, staff checked Pythius's water bowl several times to ensure it wasn't empty, and customers smiled when, having drunk his fill, he settled himself under the table like the professional pub visitor he is.

The walk

Your walk starts at the car park. On leaving it turn right into The Bank and right again into Mill Street, then walk on in this direction until you reach the B4632 which – despite being a B-road – is very busy. Caution is advised before crossing. Having crossed the road, walk 100 yards to the left until you reach a stile and a way-marker. On entering the first field, walk diagonally left until you reach another stile.

Now it is a matter of following a well-worn track, bearing slightly to the left until you come to a stile and track which bears right and takes you to yet another stile and a field leading to Queen's Wood, which will appear before you. Now cross a track, having climbed a stile on each side and enter the field that abuts the wood. This walk does not take you into the wood, instead keeping it on your right you follow its boundary

Pythius says

Helen and Uncle John think they can fool me but they can't! I knew where we were going and I also knew that there might be ghosts. Well perhaps there were but I certainly didn't see any and my fur didn't go all prickly as it does in our cottage when the lady ghosts makes one of her rare appearances. There were no phantom horses outside the pub and I didn't see anyone dressed in black lurking in the graveyard.

Poor things – Helen and Uncle John did so want me to react to a ghostly figure. They kept looking down to see if I was getting scared while I stood outside the Plough – but I wasn't! Not a single hair on my body stood on end, and I didn't feel cold or scared.

I was however, slightly concerned by the horned cattle – docile beasts though they seemed; I knew that at any time they could have stopped chewing the cud and ambled over to meet us. So was Helen, but we don't speak of that or about the field full of galloping young bullocks we met up with at the end of the walk. Gosh what a wimp Helen is at times.

and then a path which dips down past several old oak trees to a stile that returns you to the main road. As you walk this section Cheltenham's famous racecourse comes into view, also the magnificent 15th-century Tudor manor house, once the home of Lord Ellenborough, a former Governor-General of India, now the Hotel De La Bere, which like so many buildings in this area is reputed to be haunted.

Once you have crossed the road again, turn right and follow the pavement which bears left through a stylish housing estate. Soon you will spot a track on the left-hand side which leads to a gate, and then a kissing gate and a field. You will now be approaching the Hotel De La Bere on the right and be close enough to admire it properly. Perhaps, like us, you

will agree it has a slightly eerie look which suggests ghosts may be occupying some of the rooms.

At this point a well-worn track will guide you back to Prestbury, which appears on the horizon to the right. After a series of paddocks and fields you cross a footbridge and gate that would once have provided a crossing over a fast moving stream. When we stood here it was bone dry, not a spot of water to be seen.

Keeping the hedge to your right, aim for the right-hand corner of the field where you will discover yet another kissing gate and a minor road that leads to Shaw Green Lane. As you walk this lane you may encounter a ghostly rider, said to be a royal dispatch rider (we didn't). You will come to a footpath that travels through the houses and will take you back to Mill Street. You could return home at this point, or have fun wandering round Prestbury, spotting the many streets and buildings that are reputed to be haunted. These include:

Ghosts

Sundial Cottage in the Burgage where you might hear a young girl playing the spinet. As the Burgage is a medieval passage, you might well encounter a phantom with an arrow through his heart, said to appear from time to time.

Reform Cottage, Deep Street, is built alongside a monk's burial ground, so be prepared to see a ghostly monk or two.

In **Mill Street** you may well spot Mrs Pree's ghost who glides along the road towards the fields. As this street is the scene of many hauntings, you may also meet the Black Abbot wandering there, also a man dressed in a mackintosh.

Stand outside the **Plough Inn** and be prepared for the sound of horses' hooves galloping down the street. Herdsmen once found it difficult to get their sheep to pass the Plough Inn and dogs are sometimes seen to cower beside the front door.

High Street is home to a ghostly old lady in a large hat, a singing ghost and a woman in long cloths and a mob cap who glides two feet above the surface of the road.

Salford

The Black Horse

Rollright Stones

Four mile walk

There is something quite mystical about the Rollright Stones, which are listed among England's finest ancient monuments. You will find them close to a minor road off the A3400, four miles north of Chipping Norton, or by walking two miles across country from the little village of Salford.

They consist of a ceremonial stone circle dating back to 2000-2500BC, 104 feet in diameter made up of more than 70 weather-beaten oolitic limestones known as the King's Men, as well as the Whispering Knights, a group of five upright stones from the neolithic period that stand 400 yerds from the stone circle. The imposing King Stone (1800-1500BC) can be found standing in solitary splendour across the road.

It is said that however carefully you count the stones in the circle of the King's Men you will never get the same number twice.

The Black Horse

The Black Horse is an excellent place to start or finish your walk. You will find it in the small village of Salford off the busy A44, between

Chipping Norton and Moreton in Marsh.

Unfortunately food is only served here during the summer months and then only on weekdays, but they do a good line in crisps and the beer is well kept. This is one of those unpretentious little rural pubs where food doesn't count for much, but meaningful conversation and the quality of the beer does. The owners of this free house have no desire to be considered a gastro pub –

that is not their style. Obviously dogs are welcome as this is farming country and the pub attracts both farmers and their canine friends.

The walk

If you are prepared to take in Chipping Norton and Over Norton and visit St Philip's Church at Little Rollright, you can turn this into an eight mile circular walk. We usually find that a gentle two mile amble through a couple of wooded areas and several fields to get to the stones and another two miles back to Salford suits us fine.

This walk is really easy thanks to the D'arcy Dalton Way signs which stay with you until you reach the Whispering Knights. Indeed keep to this well signed path and you are almost walking in a straight line. To join this path turn right on leaving the pub and walk down the main street that curves through the village until you come to a bridleway marked Trout Lake and Rectory Farm. You can't miss it as it is at the furthermost edge of the village and lined with poplars.

Having entered the bridleway, turn left almost immediately on spotting the D'arcy Dalton Way sign which is twinned with the Shakespeare Way. This takes you over a stile and into a field which you cross diagonally, passing Rectory Farm House on your right as you do so.

One word of warning at this point; a large dog may find some of the many stiles on this walk rather difficult. We managed to squeeze Pythius through them all, but a couple did prove awkward. We got the little fellow over eventually but only after encouraging him to climb the stile as we did rather than squeezing under these awkward structures. Being the dog he is he obeyed, if somewhat reluctantly.

As waysigns will now guide you, all I need to say is follow them, they won't let you down. There are also signs requesting that dogs are kept under control and on a lead because of nesting birds and game birds in the woods – these have to be respected.

After passing through the first field, turn left and climb a couple of stiles and then bear left following the field edge until you come to a conifer wood. On leaving the trail through the wood, continue to follow the waysigns that direct you to another small wooded area and over a little stream.

You are now heading towards Manor Farm where very smart signs direct you onwards, one of which is signed to the church, the

Comptons and the Rollright Stones. You can take this path or follow the path through the farm and on ahead to a small road which will take you to the Whispering Knights. Cross the road and keep straight on over another couple of fields. Now the Whispering Knights should come into view on your left. During the winter months they are difficult to

Pythius says

I am not sure why Helen stood and stared at those funny old stones called the Whispering Knights with such interest. Apparently a witch cast a spell on them when they were real people and turned them into stone because she thought they were plotting against the King. Well – that's what Helen says and who am I to argue?

This walk was OK, if somewhat muddy in parts. There were, however, lots of times when I was put on my lead, particularly when we were walking through the farm buildings and past several enormous bulls that quite frankly terrified me – Helen too. Some of the stiles were really difficult to climb. In fact despite being a Border collie I almost got stuck when clambering over a rather tall one. Difficult that was, but I finally managed it.

spot at first as they blend in with the dark colour of the hedge. They sit hunched together some 60 yards to the left of the track and close to the field boundary and another small road. Once you have paid homage to these ancient stone relics walk on along a fenced area that will take you to the King's Men stone circle. A modest charge is made to enter this site which you are requested to put into an honesty box when the site is unattended. (These stones are open for viewing from sunrise to sunset.) You have to cross the road to bow to the magnificant King Stone who stands alone and proud.

Having found the stones, you can turn and walk back the way you came, enjoying the glorious views and the delightful sound of skylarks as the stones do stand in some breathtaking countryside; or you can continue to Little Rollright and the church, then pick up your path home from there.

Slad

The Woolpack

Laurie Lee

Circular two-and-a-half mile walk through Laurie Lee country that can be far longer if you wish

The idyllic little grey stone village of Slad, which was immortalised by Laurie Lee, nestles in the folds of the Slad valley just north of Stroud and 10 miles from Gloucester. The valley is one of those remarkably beautiful finger valleys that radiate from Stroud. The undulating landscape calls for considerable effort as you climb the hills, but be assured, it is well worth it.

You approach Slad from the tree-lined B4070 which passes through the valley. The Woolpack pub stands right in the centre close to both the old school building with its adjoining school house and the church. It is a 16th-century treasure which clings to the hillside, offering views

in abundance and an unspoiled atmosphere. Portraits of the writer Laurie Lee who gave us *Cider with Rosie* cover the walls and his collection of vintage beer bottles decorates the back of the bar. The beer pumps offer a choice of Uley beers, including Old Spot, Pig's Ear and Uley Bitter which has plenty of body and a glorious dry hoppy finish. If you are looking for a serious Cotswold ale, you can't do better than Uley, who only sell their brews to real pubs interested in the quality rather than cost-cutting discounts.

This was Laurie Lee's local. It was here that he sat enjoying the view whilst writing his notes with a pencil. Fortunately it is not a themed pub as such – but be assured his spirit fills the place.

The Woolpack is best described as unspoiled rustic and just the sort of pit stop a walker requires after climbing Swifts Hill and exploring the valley. Tables outside bring the view into focus and the intimate space inside provides conviviality and a comfortable buzz of conversation as locals chat to the walkers who pile in on a sunny day. No one could fail to be impressed by the friendly nature of this pub. The food, which includes Gloucester Old Spot sandwiches, is pretty good too.

An impressive stainless steel water bowl sits outside the main door for visiting canines who are welcome to place their paws under the tables. Pythius received several pats on the head from the locals during his visit, which pleased him greatly.

As the pub has no car park, cars have to be left alongside the road, but that is fine as it is not a very busy road and there is plenty of room.

The walk

We began by checking out Rosebank Cottage, where Laurie Lee spent his developing years with his three sisters and his mother. It is just a short walk along the road on the right-hand side and north of the pub. Unfortunately you can't view it from the front as it's built on the side of a steep bank and the steps that lead down to it are private. You can however, see clearly the T-shape of the house. Laurie and his family lived in the down-stroke. The cross-stroke was occupied by the two grannies, 'er up-a top' and 'er down under'.

Walk on a little further until you get to Stonebridge Lane on the right. It's a small road, but I'd advise you keep the dog on the lead at this point as this little lane is deceptive; many cars travel this way. Walk along the lane until you get to a restricted byway sign on the right hand side which will lead you to the pond that features in Laurie's stories. It is a rather fine pond occupied by an abundance of extremely happy ducks. Pythius certainly enjoyed it too, and as the ducks stayed in the centre of the pond nothing disastrous happened. Return to the lane after viewing the pond and walk on until you come to the second bridleway sign on the right-hand side, after admiring the posh horses in the field opposite who tolerate the company of several ducks that wander away from their pond, seeming to prefer horses and grass to a watery pond.

This is where the walk gets rather difficult as this path passes through a wooded terrain both steep and rocky. The trickles of water that fall gently over its surface mean it is also slippery and difficult to climb. But persist, despite the mud, surviving if necessary by clutching at branches either side of the path to keep you steady. The effort really is worth it. Having staggered on for a couple of hundred yards, you are looking for a crossing on this path which will take you forward and make the walk easier. Turn right when you spot two paths crossing and you are now on a smoother path, only twisted gnarled tree roots creating a slight hazard if you don't watch where you step.

You are now at the top of a hill – look down through the trees and you will see just how far up you have come. It is awesome. When the path begins to bear to the left – go with it. You will now meet up with the first of several stiles. A fading hand-painted yellow waysign points the route across a large field. This is where we got muddled for there was no exit at the other side of the field, directly opposite the sign as one would expect. On hitting a hedge we eventually turned left and followed it until we came to a metal gate and an easy-to-walk lane on the right. At this point, waysigns and stiles show you the way and things get easier. As there are several footpaths in this area you can, should you wish, now walk where you will, remembering to keep the village of Slad in your sights on the right-hand side. Return to the road and the pub is a matter of taking any one of the footpaths on the right-

Pythius says

By the time Helen and Uncle John reached that main road that runs through the village we visited, they were exhausted. They couldn't wait to get to the pub. They were elated too, because despite the various slopes they had to climb, the vistas at the top were breathtakingly beautiful. In fact at one point I heard them say this was one of the most picturesque walks they had ever experienced.

I certainly loved it, loads of amazing smells, lots of views and two lovely ponds to splash about in, even though the ducks in the first pond were rather unsociable.

The pub was superb, offering everything I needed, including companionship.

There is one thing about Helen's interest in Laurie Lee I think I ought to explain as I know she is too shy to mention it. Once, many, many years ago, apparently Laurie Lee kissed her. Yes, kissed her! She had attended the launch of Laurie Lee's collected books and was among the crowd standing in a beautiful Cotswold garden listening as he made his speech. When the speech was over and everyone began clapping, Laurie Lee stepped down from his platform and purposefully walked towards her (she was standing in the front row). Having reached her, this great man took her into his arms, gave her a big kiss and then twirled her round and round in his arms. Then, he gave her the most meaningful smile, one she says she will never forget, and then walked back to the table where he had been signing his books.

When she tells this story she says it must have been because she was wearing a home-made patchwork dress. But as it proved such a precious moment, she doesn't tell this story often.

hand side. The views now are stunning. Breathtaking actually, as they embrace the entire valley, taking in a myriad of small meadows and fields, grassy banks, hills and woods. It's possible you will sight a woodpecker and you will almost certainly hear a skylark at this point if you visit during the summer months. Kestrels are often spotted overhead too. Indeed, this is one of those magic places where nature cries out to be heard – enjoy it.

Walk on and you will probably notice that one of the meadows ahead of you has a slight yellow sheen when viewed from afar. As you walk this beautiful meadow after passing through a couple more, you will notice an abundance of wild flowers and grasses. More than 130 plant species can be found here as this is one of the meadows below Swifts Hill, part of the eastern side of the Slad valley and the Elliott

Nature Reserve. It is one of the county's finest grasslands and an important site for butterflies and wild orchids.

But first you must enter a large field and encounter the first of several posts marked with way signs that are dotted along the centre of the field. These finally lead to the yellow meadow and on to a track, past a farmhouse on your right, and a stile just a few yards round the bend. Take the second stile on the left-hand side (the first is marked private)

and walk across a well-worn path to the next stile, which sadly is not very dog-friendly due to wire netting surrounding it. We managed to get Pythius over once he had finished splashing about in a small pond beside it, but with great difficulty. Now you will find yourself in a lane that eventually leads you to a signpost to Slad Lane, the Vatch, and Stroud. The A4074 is almost immediately on your left.

At the road, put your dog on the lead, turn right and make your way back along the pavement to the pub, which is about half a mile away, for a well earned pint. Don't forget to stop off at the church to pay homage to Laurie Lee, whose gravestone states that he lies in the valley he loves. Having walked a small part of his glorious valley, I can understand why he chose this place to rest.

Snowshill Lavender Fields

A gentle trot through the lavender fields

The lavender fields were established in the year 2000 at Hill Barn Farm, Snowshill on a free draining limestone hill amid some of the most picturesque rolling countryside you could ever wish to see. When the lavender comes into bloom in June and July, this glorious 53-acre plot pulsates with colour, transforming the area into something quite magical.

As lavender comes in several different hues, including white and pink, when viewed from afar it looks as if an artist has brushed these colours onto a canvas of lush green meadows. Even if you don't walk the lavender fields, it is worth driving there to stand and stare. Besides, this area is a must if you are visiting the Cotswolds as it stands close to Broadway, Stanton, Snowshill and Ford – which rate as some of the most beautiful little villages anywhere. A visit to Cotswold Lavender can easily be incorporated into an exploration of this glorious area.

Until we walked Pythius through the fields – something that is permitted providing the dog is well behaved and on a lead – I had not realised just what a calming effect lavender can have on dogs.

We had only walked a little way along the lines of lavender plants when he stopped, turned to look at us, then sat down beside the flowers and began to sway gently from side to side with a sloppy soporific look on his face. Their fragrance was having such a calming effect on him we did wonder if he was about to curl up and go to sleep. It was all we could

Dog-friendly pubs in the area

There are three superb dog-friendly pubs no more than four miles in any direction that you can visit after viewing the Snowshill Lavender Fields.

The Plough – Ford

This gorgeous 16th-century pub, built from Cotswold stone, stands opposite the entrance to Jonjo O'Neill's famous Jackdaws Castle racing stables, so don't be surprised if you find riders in coloured silks exercising their horses on the ride alongside the Donnington Way. Decorated throughout with pictures of famous race horses, it provides a series of intimate little dining areas, a roaring log fire in the winter, and exceptionally friendly staff. This is where the racing community congregate during the Cheltenham races.

The Snowshill Arms – Snowshill

The history of this pub stretches back to the 13th century and it enjoys fantastic views of the Cotswold hills. This is one of those friendly pubs that attracts both walkers and locals. The prices are modest and the food delicious. On a sunny day it is worth enjoying your refreshments outside so that you can take in the breathtaking scenery in which the pub is set. It is close to both the Donnington and Cotswold Ways.

The Mount Inn – Stanton

As the name of this pub suggests, it has been built on a mount at the top end of one of the most beautiful villages you could wish for.

On a fine day it provides panoramic views of Evesham and the Malvern Hills. Decorated with heavy horse harnesses and dried hops which hang from its gnarled beams, it offers everything you could possibly ask from a country pub.

The food is freshly cooked to order and is scrumptious. The service is about as friendly as you can get. Dogs are very welcome – so welcome that they are even invited to use the resident dog's basket by the fire if they wish to.

Pythius says

Well, I am not sure what happened when I began walking the fields of those pretty flowers – one moment I was excited and eager to go – pulling on my lead to remind Helen it was walkie time. Then suddenly I was overcome with

a powerful desire to sleep. Perhaps I would have done so if Helen hadn't called me to attention. I've never experienced anything quite like that before; I am usually really alert when we explore new territory, but this time I felt so calm and relaxed. As I breathed in that wonderful aroma coming from the flowers I just wanted to curl up and sleep. Now I smell this scent in the cottage sometimes and I am not sure why and when Helen bakes scones I have noticed she sometimes adds a pinch of lavender flowers to the mixture.

---

do to refrain from laughing, but as you should never laugh at dogs (they can't cope with it), we controlled our urge to do anything more than smile, though the people walking nearby did laugh, and loudly. As they weren't making eye contact with him, the poor creature just went on swaying. Whilst I can't guarantee that your dog will react this way, I can assure you that the jar of lavender we bought from the little shop at the farm calms him too. And if I spray lavender essence around the cottage, he curls up and goes to sleep.

The attractive shop and tea room adjacent to the lavender fields was built from an old stable and fodder store. It is open from 10 am to 5 pm and serves refreshments until 4.30 pm. Lavender plants and products are on sale here too. Unfortunately dogs are not allowed in the shop.

However, should you wish, you can let your dog follow each line of lavender plants and walk up and down for more than 50 miles in total – we didn't go that far. I doubt Pythius would have stayed awake that long.

Swinbrook

The Swan Inn

A two-mile river walk in the footsteps of the Mitford sisters

It's hard to imagine a more beautiful setting for a country inn than Swinbrook, a small Cotswold village unravished by time, just two miles east of Burford, which boasts a traditional cricket ground with wooden pavilion, a 12th-century church and a delightful stone bridge that spans the River Windrush opposite the Swan Inn. Only the occasional passing car acts as a reminder that you are in the 21st century.

Just half a mile away is Asthall Manor where the Mitfords once lived, but Swinbrook is also the Mitford sisters' territory as becomes clear the moment you enter the Swan and see the collection of sepia photographs that adorn its walls. There they all are, Nancy, Pamela, Diana, Unity, Jessica and Deborah – the six daughters of David Freeman-Mitford, 2nd Baron Redesdale, known collectively as the Mitford Sisters. Images of this remarkable sextet of celebrities can be viewed linking arms for a group photograph, visiting the henhouse for a fresh clutch of eggs, riding to hounds and hugging their pet dogs. It's no wonder that the collection appears to favour Deborah, the baby of the family – now the Dowager Duchess of Devonshire – as she owns the Swan and still takes an active interest in the inn which is in the capable hands of Archie Orr-Ewing, who also runs the King's Head, Bledington. A room is always kept for her use in the row of recently built bedrooms at the back of the pub.

Scrubbed oak tables and smiling bar staff also help set the scene and a well-balanced seasonal menu offering sandwiches, soup and main meals will gladden your heart, as most ingredients are sourced locally. The food here is not cheap, but it is perfectly cooked, offering guests exactly what they have paid for. Water for visiting canines is freely available. They usually get a pat on the head too.

Surrounded by images of smiling sisters in their country tweeds, you will find it easy to imagine them walking along the banks of the Windrush, fishing for trout with their father, visiting the local church and skipping arm in arm through the surrounding fields in the beautiful Windrush Valley. Asthall Manor where they lived during their childhood is just half a mile away.

The Mitford sisters

Nancy: the eldest of six children. She found success with her fifth novel *The Pursuit of Love* and its sequel *Love in a Cold Climate*.

Pamela: known as the woman who developed a deep love of the countryside and went on to become a poultry expert.

Diana: considered the most classically beautiful, who married Bryan Guinness, heir to the Guinness brewery fortune, though she was in love with Sir Oswald Mosley, whom she married when his first wife died.

Unity: a rather boisterous teenager who became a fascist and a member of Hitler's social circle. She tried to commit suicide by shooting herself in the head on hearing that England was at war with Germany.

Jessica: the communist who disliked her upbringing so much she placed her pocket money into a 'running away' account. She emigrated to America where she wrote a series of attacks on the establishment.

Deborah: known as Debo, she was far less competitive than her sisters. Married Andrew Cavendish, the younger son of the Duke of Devonshire and did much to restore the neglected family estate of Chatworth.

Tom: The only boy of the family. He became a lawyer.

The walk

Two walks begin at the Swan. You can go across fields towards Asthall and the Maytime Inn past the Mitfords' manor house and then follow the road back to Swinbrook. Or turn left on leaving the Swan Inn and head down a minor road toward the main village of Swinbrook and the village green. Walk through the gated footpath besides St Mary's Church on the left, turning right at the end of the

---

Pythius says

I have studied the photographs hanging on the walls of the Swan Inn; it seems that the sisters that intrigue Helen so were very fond of dogs. This must mean they were nice people, even though a couple of them knew Mr Hitler. Terrific pub, I am allowed to sit wherever I want to and the walk is great except when there are often cows in the field by the little church. That's when Helen usually turns round and goes the other way – I don't know why.

---

path and following the track that leads you to towards the little church of St Oswald that dates from 660AD. This remarkable little church with its Victorian wooden box pews sits in the middle of a field and offers you a chance to admire faded murals painted there after the Black Death decimated the population of the lost village of Widford. This is the walk we prefer.

Undulations in the field in which St Oswald's stands indicate that domestic dwellings once surrounded the church. On leaving the church, turn left and then left again up the secluded valley before you. Walk on until you come to a farm gate leading to a country lane. Turn right and walk on uphill until you come to a restricted path, and follow this downward sloping track until you reach another farm gate. Continue an uphill climb through the pasture, which puts part of the royal hunting forest of Wychwood on your left and offers a spectacular view of the surrounding countryside on your right. Pass through another (the last) farm gate and follow the dry stone wall to Pain's farm

where you will see an old duck pond that filters water collected from the hills into a lovely little stream. On turning right onto a paved country lane, you soon reach a junction sign that points you back to Swinbrook, reached by walking a charming country lane.

If you take both walks you will have covered about three miles.

Upper Slaughter
The Lords of the Manor

Two-mile walk along the Warden's Way to Lower Slaughter and back

Pythius says:

Helen has allowed me to write the introduction to the hotel we visited this time after I'd pointed out that it should be seen entirely from a dog's point of view. So here we go.

Every now and again Helen likes to go 'posh' and visit a stylish pub or hotel for a mini break. This is why I found myself having to suffer the indignities of a bath and discovered her packing my feeding bowl and a bag of doggie food into an overnight case the other day.

She had decided that we should have an overnight stay in a Michelin-starred hotel – The Lords of the Manor at Upper Slaughter, where dogs are not just welcome, but VERY welcome. Indeed they are treated as honoured guests.

We have visited this glorious country hotel for lunch often, but this was different, we were not just going for lunch but for a whole night away from home. I am not sure which of us was more excited once I had got over the experience of being dumped in the bath and covered with shampoo.

Helen was looking forward to a gourmet dinner that night, cooked by a very talented team of chefs. Sadly she believes I should have a regular diet, so I was only going to get my normal tin of Butcher's dog food with four handfuls of dog meal mixed into it – but that is my only complaint. That said, I was excited too as this is the hotel where guests can ask the concierge to walk their dogs round the lake at the bottom of the garden first thing in the morning while their masters are enjoying a "posh," early morning bath before breakfast.

As dogs are not allowed in the dining room (the only place they are refused entry) Helen and I ate breakfast outside in the garden after I'd had my walk round the lake with that lovely man who likes Border collies. Helen admits that she could have easily walked me herself, but she wanted me to enjoy the full-hotel-experience and I did. I have never been walked by a man in uniform before and admit I rather liked the fact he called me "Sir". He even asked me which way round the lake I would like to walk, and brushed me down before returning me to our room. And what a room it was, all beautifully furnished in a way that was both comfortable and stylish. Helen had packed my rug, so I was able to snuggle down beside her bed during the night. That was nice and stopped me getting homesick.

The walk

Having enjoyed a superb breakfast eaten in the sunshine amid roses in full bloom, lavender and herbs, Pythius and I set out for the picturesque village of Lower Slaughter. Lower and Upper Slaughter are the two villages that the writer J.B. Priestley described as two symphonies of grey stone that should be preserved for ever as they are now. I am inclined to agree.

On leaving the hotel we turned right and followed the path for about a hundred yards, taking the right-hand lane that is marked the Warden's Way. This took us down a curving fenced path to a small bridge crossing the River Eye and a gate that opens up into a large field. At this point the way-markers you need to follow have a small W marked in green to indicate you are following the Warden's Way. This is really all you need to know as the path has been clearly mapped out by the hundreds of footsteps that have gone before you. It's a walk to take at a leisurely pace so that the undulating landscape decorated with an ancient breed of sheep can be enjoyed.

Unfortunately the presence of sheep meant that Pythius had to remain on his lead as we passed them. You will frequently find requests to keep dogs under control as you make this mile-long walk. Such

requests have to be respected. As several of the fields are devoid of sheep, there were moments when he was free to walk beside me without restraint. He enjoyed that.

On reaching Lower Slaughter, we made our way to the tall red-brick Victorian chimney of the Old Mill, which is now a well-stocked craft-shop with a riverside café. Here we relaxed for a few moments. Pythius was served a bowl of water and I enjoyed a cup of freshly brewed coffee and a scrumptious slice of hand-made chocolate cake while we relaxed and watched the river flow gently by. What a glorious feeling that is. There we were in the most picturesque setting, doing nothing more than watching and listening as the river rippled gently by. The many ducks and swans that inhabit the river added that extra something to this glorious experience.

The Warden's Way – leading us back the way we came – is sign-posted next to the Mill, so all we had to do was return the way we had come, greet the sheep that have a black stripe running down under the bellies, listen to the squawking rooks that nest high in the trees and enjoy the scenery which is breathtaking. It took no time at all for us to spot The Lords of the Manor, looking as if it was emerging from the very earth on which it was planted.

The Lords of the Manor

Formerly an old rectory, this privately-owned 17th-century country hotel is situated in an idyllic corner of the Cotswolds close to the A429 and only a couple of miles from Bourton-on-the-Water. Nice little touches that really make you feel every need is being catered for include the Wellington boots left by the front door should guests require them. It goes without saying that this elegant establishment serves superb food and excellent wine. Dogs stay for free!

Pythius' Epilogue

I have been helping Helen write the Paws books since her retirement from The Oxford Times office and must admit it has not always been easy. Helen is a hard taskmistress, often insisting that we walk on a cold, wet day because she wants to explore more of the Cotswolds, when I would rather snuggle up in my basket. She wins these arguments of course, and I am pleased she does. The Cotswolds are simply amazing, regardless of weather conditions. In fact there are times during the frosty winter months when my heart sings with joy at the thought of running free across such a glorious landscape.

Helen says that our exploration of the Cotswolds has only scratched the surface, and there is much we still haven't seen or mentioned, which suggests she is going to continue her quest to know the area better. She mentions the fact that we have not walked in Elgar's foot-steps yet. She also wants to visit Pershore during its autumn Plum Festival and the Vale of Evesham when asparagus comes into season. The Dover's Hill Olimpick Games at Chipping Campden is also on her list of things to do, so I guess our adventures with Auntie Liz, Uncle John and Auntie Caroline will continue for as long as I have the strength to follow her.

I just hope that our walks have inspired other dog-owners to visit the Cotswolds and walk those secluded valleys and floral meadows that I have grown to love so much.

I am indeed a very lucky dog.

Pythius Peacocke

Contact Information

Batsford Arboretum – 01386 701441 – www.batsarb.co.uk

Bibury – The Catherine Wheel – 01285 740250 – www.catherinewheel-bibury.co.uk

Bredon Hill – The Star Inn, Ashton Under Hill – 01386 881325 –
www.thestar-ashtonunderhill.co.uk

Broadway Tower – Morris and Brown – 01386 852945 – www.morrisandbrown.co.uk

Chedworth – Seven Tuns – 01285 720242 – email theseventuns@clara.co.uk

Cotswold Wildlife Park – 01993 823006 – www.cotswoldwildlifepark.co.uk

Cranhan – The Black Horse – 01452 812217 –
www.theblackhorsecranham.co.uk

Down Ampney – Old Spotted Cow (Marston Meysey) – 01285 810264 –
www.theoldspottedcow.co.uk

Ducklington – The Bell – 01993 706822

Enstone – The Crown Inn – 01608 677262

Filkins – The Five Alls – 01367 860875 – www.thefiveallsfilkins.co.uk

Finstock – The Plough Inn – 01993 868333 – www.theplough-inn.co.uk

Fossebridge – The Inn at Fossebridge – 01285 720721 –
www.fossebridgeinn.co.uk

Hailes Abbey – 01242 602398 & Farmcote Chilli Farm – 01242 603860 –
www.farmcoteherbs.co.uk

Kelmscott – The Plough – 01367 253543 – www.ploughkelmscott.com

King's Stanley – The King's Head – 01453 828293

Lechlade – The Riverside – 01367 252534 – www.riverside-lechlade.com

Lower Oddington – The Fox Inn – 01451 870555 – www.foxinn.net

Malmesbury – The Smoking Dog – 01666 825823 – www.sabrain.com/smoking dog

May Hill – The Yew Tree, Cliffords Mesne – 01531 820719 –
www.yewtreeinn.com

Minster Lovell – The Old Swan and Minster Mill – 01993 774441 –
www.oldswanandminstermill.com

Moreton in Marsh – The Bell Inn – 01608 651688 – www.thebellatmoreton.co.uk

Nether Westcote – 01993 833030 – www.thefeatherednestinn.co.uk

Nympsfield – 01453 860240 – www.theroseandcrowninn.com

Ozleworth – (No pub mentioned in this chapter)

Prestbury – The Plough Inn – 01242 222180 – www.ploughprestbury.co.uk

Slad – The Woolpack Inn – 01452 813429

Snowshill Lavender – 01386 854821 – www.cotswoldlavender.co.uk

Stichcombe Hill – The Old Spot – 01453 542870 – www.oldspotinn.co.uk

Swinbrook – The Swan Inn – 01993 823339 – www.theswanswinbrook.co.uk

Upper Slaughter – Lords of the Manor – 01451 820243 – www.lordsofthemanor.com